KU-176-311

New advanced vocabulary
Wort für Wort
German

Paul Stocker

Hodder & Stoughton
A MEMBER OF THE HODDER HEADLINE GROUP

Acknowledgements

I should like to thank Martin Fries for checking the typescript, and for his useful suggestions; and my family for being patient most of the time.

Orders: please contact Bookpoint Ltd, 39 Milton Park, Abingdon, Oxon OX14 4TD. Telephone: (44) 01235 400414, Fax: (44) 01235 400454. Lines are open from 9.00–6.00, Monday to Saturday, with a 24 hour message answering service. E-mail address: orders@bookpoint.co.uk

British Library Cataloguing in Publication Data
A catalogue entry for this title is available from the British Library

ISBN 0 340 77163 1

First published 1992
Second edition 1996
Third edition 2000
Impression number 10 9 8 7 6 5 4 3 2
Year   2004 2003 2002 2001

Typeset by Transet Limited, Coventry, England
Printed in Great Britain for Hodder and Stoughton Educational, a division of Hodder Headline Plc, 338 Euston Road, London NW1 3BH

Introduction

Who is this book for?

As a student of a foreign language you probably wish to move beyond everyday and transactional matters, and to read, talk or write about a wide range of issues such as technology, the arts, or the world of work. This book is intended for you, and in particular for those of you taking courses in German beyond beginner level. Much of the vocabulary has been drawn from the internet, newspapers, and magazines to ensure that it is in current use.

How the book is set out

The sections within each unit are, where appropriate, divided into short sub-sections; within these, items are grouped by sense, rather than in alphabetical order, which tends to separate even closely-related items in an apparently arbitrary way. Often, words are given in phrases to provide a context and a 'feel' for the way language is used; you can, of course, extract individual nouns or verbs from this to use in a different context.

- Unit 1 Ich meine lists words and short phrases for use in discussions (section A), then longer items for use in written work (section B)
- Unit 18 Welches Wort soll ich wählen? lists key words for which English speakers often find it difficult to select the most appropriate German equivalent.

At the end of each unit you will find a selection of related **websites**, which will provide up-to-date information in German or help you to extend your vocabulary further.

Learning vocabulary

Building one's active vocabulary quickly and efficiently (which also means *remembering* it!) is a major concern. Here is one technique for doing so. Always learn vocabulary at the beginning of a homework session while you are still fresh.

1. Sit in a quiet place. No background music for this work!
2. Read each German–English pair of words or phrases **aloud, twice,** concentrating hard on the spelling as you do so.
3. After five pairs, cover up the English side of the page, and repeat the five pairs aloud again.
4. As stage 3, but this time cover the German side. Write the words out.
5. After 20 pairs, repeat stage 4. Repeat stages 3 and 4 after 2 hours, and again the next day. Give yourself a written test.

With practice, you will be able to learn 20–30 words in 10–15 minutes, and remember almost all of them weeks later.

Developing your vocabulary

Language is constantly changing. Jot down new words and expressions as you hear or read them. Note which verbs/nouns/prepositions are combined with each item. Try to use the items in conversation or writing while they are still fresh.

Abbreviations used in this book

Acc	Accusative
adj. noun	noun which works like an adjective
conj	conjunction
Dat	Dative
etw.	*etwas*
fem	feminine
Gen	Genitive
inf	informal, colloquial
insep	inseparable verb
invar	invariable case ending
irreg	irregular verb
itr	intransitive verb
jn.	*jemanden*; shows that the verb or preposition takes the accusative
jm.	*jemandem*; shows that the verb or preposition takes the dative
masc	masculine
nt	neuter
o.s.	oneself
pej	pejorative
pl	plural
sing	singular
s.o.	someone
sth.	something
tr	transitive
*	perfect tense formed with *sein*

- The vowel changes of less common strong verbs are given in brackets after the infinitive e.g. *treten (i-a-e)*
- Feminine forms of professions etc. are, for simplicity's sake, only included where they vary from the usual addition of *-in* to the masculine form.

Paul Stocker

Contents

www.yahoo.de   *search-engine*
www.dino-online.de   *search engine*
www.statistik-bund.de   *Statistical information on many aspects of German life*
www.lbb.bw.schule.de   *Links to social, political, legal, economic sites*
www.inter-nationes.de
www.linguanet.org.uk

Einfache Ausdrücke | Simple expressions

1 Ideen ordnen — *Ordering ideas*

erstens, zunächst	first/ly
zweitens	secondly
am Anfang/zu Anfang	initially
später	later
schließlich	finally
von vorn	from scratch, from the beginning
endlich	at last
zum Abschluss	in conclusion

2 Ideen hinzufügen — *Adding ideas*

auch	also
dazu	in addition
nicht nur ..., sondern auch ...	not only ..., but also ...
außerdem	moreover
übrigens	incidentally, by the way
und dazu kommt noch, dass ... weiter	and, what is more, ...
natürlich	of course
was ich eigentlich sagen wollte, ist ...	what I actually mean is ...

3 Beispiele geben — *Giving examples*

zum Beispiel (z.B.) beispielsweise	for example (e.g.)
bekanntlich	it is known that
folgendermaßen	as follows
das heißt (d.h.)	that is (i.e.)
wie	such as
es stimmt, dass ...	it is true that ...
in diesem Zusammenhang	in this context
nämlich	viz., namely
in Bezug auf (+Acc)	with reference to
unter anderem (u.a.)	among other things

4 Ursache und Wirkung — *Cause and effect*

folglich	consequently, as a result

dadurch, deshalb, deswegen	in that way, because of that, that is why
daher	thus
also	therefore, so
da (*conj.*)	since, as
weil (*conj.*)	because
schon weil ...	if only because ...
schon die Tatsache, dass ...	the very fact that ...
solange (*conj.*)	as/so long as
soweit ich weiß	as/so far as I know
das liegt daran, dass ...	that's because ...

5 Bestimmte Aspekte betonen

Emphasising certain aspects

es steht fest, dass ...	what is sure is that ...
ausgerechnet wenn/als ...	just when ...
ausgerechnet er	he of all people
vor allem	above all, notably
ausnahmslos	without exception
durchaus	absolutely, definitely
äußerst	extremely
ganz und gar	completely, utterly
bei weitem (das Beste)	by far and away (the best)
bei weitem (nicht so gut wie)	nowhere near (as good as)
in jeder Hinsicht	in every respect
keineswegs	not at all, not in the least
eben; halt	just, simply
besonders; zumal	in particular; especially as
genau das	especially this
hauptsächlich	notably, mainly
noch (bedeutender)	(even) more (significantly)
um so mehr, als	all the more, considering/as
um so wichtiger	all the more important
sogar	even (*intensifier*)
möglichst (bald)	as (soon) as possible
(das musst du) unbedingt (machen)	(you) really (must do that)
völlig, vollkommen	completely
unbestritten ist, dass ...	it's not disputed that ...

6 Zweifel ausdrücken

Expressing reservations

angeblich	supposedly, allegedly
abgesehen davon, dass ...	quite apart from the fact that ...

allenfalls; bestenfalls	at best
allerdings	even so/mind you
bis zu einem gewissen Grade	to some extent
einigermaßen	
es sei denn, ...	unless
gewissermaßen	in a way
kaum	hardly
keinesfalls	under no circumstances
ich habe den Eindruck, dass ...	my impression is that ...
es kommt darauf an, was ...	it depends on what ...
da habe ich Zweifel	I have my doubts there
lediglich	merely, simply
praktisch; quasi	virtual(-ly)
relativ	relatively
selbst wenn	even if
teilweise	partly
vermutlich	presumably
auf den ersten Blick	at first sight
wie kommst du darauf?	what makes you think that?

7 Ideen vergleichen
Comparing ideas

genauso	just the same
genauso wichtig	just as important
ähnlich (+Dat)	similar to, like
ebenso	likewise
sowie	as well as
im Vergleich zu (+Dat)	(when) compared with
verglichen mit (+Dat)	
kannst du das näher erklären?	can you explain that more fully?
was sagst du zum Problem von ...?	what's your view on the problem of ...?
welche Einstellung hast du zu ...?	what's your attitude to ...?
wie ist deine Meinung?	what's your opinion?
als je zuvor	than ever before

8 Der andere Standpunkt
Contrasting opinion

das hat damit nichts zu tun	that has nothing to do with it
in Wirklichkeit	in reality, in actual fact
aber/jedoch	however
trotz (+Gen or Dat)	in spite of
außer (+Dat)	apart from

immerhin	all the same
in der Tat	in fact
zugegeben; zwar	admittedly
doch	however/though/ (and to contradict a negative question or statement)
da haben Sie schon recht, aber (*inf*)	you *are* right there, but ...
wohl, aber ...	that may well be, but ...
na schön, aber ...	that's all very well, but ...
wer das glaubt, ...	anyone who believes that ...
als Alternative	alternatively
im Gegenteil	on the contrary
das stimmt auf keinen Fall	that's absolutely untrue
einerseits; andererseits	on the one/other hand
auf der einen/anderen Seite	on the one/other hand
dagegen	on the other hand
mag sein, aber ... (*inf*)	that may well be, but ...
das ist aus der Luft gegriffen	that's nothing to do with the facts
obwohl (*conj.*)	although
überhaupt	anyway
trotzdem; dennoch	nevertheless, despite this
was ... angeht,	as for ...,
es ist fraglich, ob ...	it's questionable whether ...
es ist unvorstellbar, dass ...	it's inconceivable that ...
statt dessen	instead
während (*conj.*)	whereas
sonst	otherwise
es kann sein, dass ...	it may be true that ...
egal ob ...	it doesn't matter whether ...
dabei	at the same time/into the bargain
problematisch dabei ist ...	the problem with it is ...
dafür	in return
freilich	admittedly
praktisch/in der Praxis	in practice

9 Meinungen äußern

Expressing opinions

du musst doch einsehen, dass ...	you must agree that ...
natürlich selbstverständlich }	of course

zweifellos	doubtless
daran gibt es keinen Zweifel	there can be no doubt about that
ohne Zweifel	undeniably
klar	clearly
sicher	certainly
es steht fest, dass ...	it is certain that ...
es liegt auf der Hand, dass ... es versteht sich von selbst, dass ... }	it is obvious that ...
offensichtlich	evidently
es geht um (+Acc)	it is a question of sth.
es geht darum, ob ...	it is a question of whether
kurz gesagt	in brief
kurz und gut	in a nutshell
im Großen und Ganzen	on the whole
größtenteils	in the main
im Allgemeinen	in general
im Grunde	basically
in der Regel	as a rule

10 Schlüsse ziehen *Drawing conclusions*

zum Schluss	in conclusion
es scheint, als ob ...	it would seem that ...
mir scheint es so, dass ...	it seems to me that ...
es ist alles andere als ...	it is anything but ...
ich bin davon überzeugt, dass ...	I'm convinced that ...
schlicht und einfach	plainly and simply
ich schlage vor, (dass ...)	I suggest (that ...)
glücklicherweise	fortunately
leider	unfortunately
es ist schade, dass ...	it is a pity that ...
es ist unbegreiflich, dass ...	it is inconceivable that ...
ohnehin	anyway
ehrlich gesagt	to be honest with you
meiner Meinung nach	in my opinion
ganz meine Meinung!	that's just what I think!
genau!	exactly!
so ist es! }	that's right!
das sag ich auch!	I think so too!
offen gestanden	quite frankly

11 Weitere nützliche Ausdrücke *Other useful phrases*

an sich	actually, on the whole

5

dadurch	in that way, because of that
dafür	in return, in exchange
gelegentlich	occasionally
leider	unfortunately
irgendjemand	someone or other
irgendwann	(at) some time or other
irgendwas	something (or other)
irgendwie	somehow (or other)
irgendwo(-hin)	(to) somewhere or other
meistens	mostly, more often than not
mindestens	at least
normalerweise	usually
ohne weiteres	straight away, without a second thought
nach und nach	bit by bit
sozusagen	so to speak
stellenweise	in places, here and there
teilweise	partly, in part
übrigens	incidentally
unerhört	incredible, outrageous
ungewöhnlich	unusual(-ly)
vermutlich	presumably
vielleicht	perhaps
wahrscheinlich	probably
weitgehend	largely
was ... betrifft	as far as ... is concerned

B

Längere Ausdrücke	**Longer phrases**
1 Einleitung	*Introduction*
Ist das zu rechtfertigen?	can this be justified?
das Pro und Contra } das Für und Wider }	the pros and cons
angenommen, dass ...	assuming that ...
in vieler Hinsicht	in many respects
man gewinnt häufig den Eindruck, dass ...	one often gets the impression that
man könnte meinen, dass ...	one might think that ...
gehen wir davon aus, dass ...	let's assume that ...
es wird zu oft von anderen Themen in den Hintergrund gedrängt	it is often pushed into the background by the other issues

es ist zum Thema geworden	it has become an issue
ein umstrittenes Problem	a controversial issue
eine heikle Frage	a thorny question
darüber wird heftig diskutiert	it has provoked a lot of discussion
ein nicht zu unterschätzendes Problem	a problem which should not be underestimated
es geht uns alle an	it concerns us all
eine heftige öffentliche Diskussion auslösen	to arouse intense public debate
die Meinungen über ... (+Acc) gehen weit auseinander	opinions about ... differ widely
alle sind sich darüber einig, dass ...	everyone is agreed that ...
die Auseinandersetzung über ... (+Acc)	the argument about ...
wir müssen uns damit auseinander setzen, was ...	we must tackle the problem of what ...
an dieser vieldiskutierten Frage scheiden sich die Geister	opinions are divided on this vexed question
plädieren für (+Acc)	to speak up for ...
Kritiker bemängeln, dass ...	critics point out that ...

2 These

Arguments for

wir dürfen nicht vergessen, dass ...	we must not forget that ...
was Sorgen bereiten sollte, ist ...	what should cause concern is ...
die Folgen werden leicht unterschätzt	it is easy to underestimate the consequences
es ist leicht zu ersehen, dass ...	it is easy to see that ...
es wird zunehmend erkannt, dass ...	it is increasingly being recognised that ...
das muss man als wichtiges Anliegen erkennen	this must be recognised as an important area of concern
etwas stimmt nicht mit ... (+Dat)	there's something wrong with ...
das Problem hat beängstigende Ausmaße erreicht	the problem has reached worrying proportions
die Lage wird schlechter	the situation is getting worse
– erregt weiterhin Besorgnis (-se)	– continues to cause concern
– wird durch ... erschwert	– is made worse by ...
vom politischen Standpunkt aus gesehen	from the political point of view
es ist nicht zu leugnen, dass ...	one cannot deny that ...
es steht außer Zweifel, dass ...	it is beyond doubt that

das Auffallende ist, dass …	the striking thing is that …
wir legen zu viel Wert auf (+Acc)	we attach too much importance to …
dank (+Gen or Dat)	thanks to
darauf wollen wir später zurückkommen	we shall return to this later
auf Widerstand stoßen (ö-ie-o)	to meet with resistance
auf viel Kritik stoßen (ö-ie-o)	to encounter a great deal of criticism
die Sache auf die Spitze treiben	to bring matters to a head

3 Antithese — *Arguments against*

er geht von falschen Voraussetzungen aus	he is arguing from false assumptions
die Sache hat einen Haken	there is a snag
wenn wir es genauer betrachten	if we look at it more closely
dieser Auffassung kann ich nicht zustimmen	I cannot accept this view
ganz abgesehen davon …	quite apart from that …
wir können uns der Tatsache nicht verschließen, dass …	we cannot ignore the fact that …
dagegen lässt sich einwenden, dass …	one objection to this is that …
im Gegenteil	on the contrary
einer (Dat) Sache im Weg stehen	to be a stumbling block
der Sündenbock	scapegoat
das ist nur selten der Fall	that is only rarely the case
es fehlt oft an (+Dat)	there is often a lack of
es kann leicht vorkommen, dass …	it can easily happen that …
es erwies sich als falsch	it turned out to be wrong
das sollte man mit einem gewissen Argwohn betrachten	one should view this with some mistrust
seine Argumente kann man nicht für bare Münze nehmen	you can't take his arguments at face value
es gibt keinen Anlass zu (+Dat) …	there are no grounds for …
das ist zum Scheitern verurteilt	it is condemned to failure
die Gründe sind noch nicht endgültig geklärt	the reasons have not been fully explained
dies will nicht heißen, dass …	this does not mean that …
geschweige denn …	not to mention …
allerdings sollte man …	however, we should …
man könnte annehmen, dass …	it might be assumed that …

4 Gründe geben

Giving reasons

die Zahl wird auf ... geschätzt	the number is estimated at ...
es wird geschätzt, dass ...	it is estimated that ...
es ist erwiesen, dass ...	it is a proven fact that ...
nach fachmännischen Schätzungen	according to expert estimates
laut Bundeskanzler	according to the Prime Minister
laut (+Gen or Dat) Gesetz	according to the law
nach Erkenntnissen (+Gen) ...	according to the findings of ...
aus folgenden Gründen	for the following reasons
aus politischen Gründen	for political reasons
aus diesem Grund	for that reason
wie oben erwähnt	as mentioned above
die Statistik macht deutlich, dass ...	the statistics show clearly that ...
in dieser/mancher Hinsicht	in this/many respect(s)
aller Wahrscheinlichkeit nach	by the law of averages/in all probability
gelten (i-a-o) für	to be true of
man vergleiche ...	let us compare
um ein einziges Beispiel zu nennen	to take a single example
das kann man an einem Beispiel klarmachen/belegen	an example will illustrate this
das gilt auch für ...	the same is also true of ...
man muss darauf hinweisen, dass ...	one must point out that ...

5 Schlussfolgerungen ziehen

Drawing conclusions

das hat zur Folge, (dass ...)	the effect of that (is that ...)
man kommt unweigerlich zu dem Schluss, dass ...	one is forced to the conclusion that ...
es lässt sich daraus schließen, dass ...	we can conclude from that that ...
ich bin davon überzeugt, dass ...	I am convinced that ...
wenn man alles in Betracht zieht } alles in allem	all things considered
das kleinere Übel	the lesser evil
die Stichhaltigkeit des Arguments	the validity of the argument
die Aufgabe ist es/besteht darin ...	the task is, ...
um dieses Ziel zu erreichen	to achieve this goal
ein Ziel im Auge behalten	to keep an aim in mind
einfache Lösungen gibt es nicht	there are no easy solutions
zum Scheitern verurteilt	condemned to failure
wir können uns dem Problem nicht verschließen	we cannot ignore the problem

9

diese Einzelmaßnahmen müssen mit ... (+*Dat*) gekoppelt sein	these individual measures must be linked to ...
um diesen Gefahren vorzubeugen	in order to avert these dangers
die richtigen Prioritäten setzen	to get one's priorities right
das ist erst möglich, wenn ...	that is only possible if ...
es verlangt eine Umstellung unserer Einstellungen	it demands a change in our attitudes
ich bin der Ansicht, dass ...	I think that ...
es bleibt uns nichts Anderes übrig, als ...	we have no alternative but to ...
man sollte sich vor Augen halten, dass ...	we should not lose sight of the fact that ...
das Entscheidende dabei ist ...	the decisive factor in this is ...

Zeitausdrücke

Time

1 Die Vergangenheit

The past

anno dazumal	in the old days
in den letzten paar Jahren	in the last few years
in der guten alten Zeit	in the good old days
in letzter Zeit	recently (*up to now*)
neulich	recently (*not very long ago*)
damals	in those days
bis jetzt	until now
bis vor kurzem	until recently
seit ewigen Zeiten	for ages
längst	for a long time (past)
das ist schon seit jeher so	it's always been like that
zu der Zeit, als ...	at a time when ...
von Anfang an	right from the start
vor mehreren Jahren	several years ago
erst gestern	not until/only yesterday
1999/im Jahr 1999	in 1999
in den 70er Jahren	in the seventies

2 Die Gegenwart

The present

mit der Zeit gehen	to move with the times
heutzutage	nowadays
momentan	at present
in den neunziger Jahren	in the nineties
im neuen Jahrtausend	in the new millennium

im Anfangsstadium	in the early stages
gleichzeitig	at the same time
vorläufig	for the time being
inzwischen	in the meantime
aktuell	up-to-date, current
in der Nacht zum 24. Juli	on the night of the 23rd July
es ist höchste Zeit, dass ...	it's high time that ...

3 Die Zukunft
The future

in der Zukunft	in days to come
von jetzt an/in Zukunft	from now on/in future
für alle Zeiten	for all time
auf unbestimmte Zeit	for an indefinite period of time
mit der Zeit	in (the course of) time
früher oder später	sooner or later
über Nacht	overnight
möglichst bald	as soon as possible
im Voraus	in advance
vorzeitig	ahead of time
Versäumtes aufholen	to make up for lost time

4 Weitere nützliche Ausdrücke
Other useful phrases

alle 10 Minuten	every 10 minutes
jede halbe Stunde	every half an hour
jeden zweiten Tag	every other day
immer wieder	again and again
fast die ganze Zeit	most of the time
zu jeder Zeit	at any time
das ganze Jahr über	all year round
den ganzen Tag	all day
tagaus, tagein	day in, day out
zum ersten Mal	for the first time
die Altersgruppe (-n)	age group
er ist in den Vierzigern	he's in his forties
sie ist Anfang/Ende zwanzig	she's in her early/late twenties
in den mittleren Jahren	middle-aged
mit den Jahren	as one gets older
nach und nach	bit by bit, gradually

www.iicm.edu/ref.m10   Meyer's Lexikon

Die Liebe

jn. auf einer Party kennen lernen	to meet s.o. at a party
sich in jn. verlieben	to fall in love with s.o.
sich bis über beide Ohren in jn. verlieben	to fall head over heels in love
die Liebe auf den ersten Blick	love at first sight
in jm. vernarrt sein	to be infatuated with s.o.
mit jm. flirten	to flirt with s.o.
der Traummann/die Traumfrau	ideal partner
an seinen Partner hohe Ansprüche stellen	to demand high standards of one's partner
jn. um den kleinen Finger wickeln	to wrap s.o. round one's little finger
jn. anquatschen/anmachen	to chat s.o. up
ein Mädchen ansprechen	to talk to a girl
anziehend, reizend	attractive
braungebrannt	bronzed
mit jm. gehen	to go out with s.o.
mit jm. ausgehen	to take s.o. out
mit jm. Schluss machen	to finish with s.o.
sich einen Korb holen	to get the push

Die Ehe — Marriage

ledig	single
verheiratet	married
sich verloben mit	to get engaged to
die Verlobung	engagement
heiraten	to get married
die Hochzeit	wedding
die standesamtliche Trauung	civil ceremony
die Braut	bride
der Bräutigam	groom
das Ehepaar (-e)	married couple
der Ehemann (-̈er)	husband
die Ehefrau (-en)	wife
der Lebensgefährte/die Lebensgefährtin	partner/common-law husband/wife
der Polterabend	pre-wedding party

zusammenleben	to live together
mit jm. schlafen	to make love
das gegenseitige Verständnis	mutual understanding
sich verstehen	to get on well with each other
die Gemeinsamkeit	common ground
sie haben vieles gemeinsam	they have a lot in common
man soll über alles sprechen können	you should be able to talk about everything
die Zärtlichkeit	tenderness
das Vertrauen	trust

Trennung, Scheidung, Tod — Separation, divorce, death

er will sich nicht gebunden fühlen	he doesn't want any ties
der Seitensprung (¨e)	affair outside marriage
fremdgehen	to have affairs
sie leben getrennt	they live apart
Ehebruch begehen	to commit adultery
ihre Ehe ging in die Brüche	their marriage broke up
die Scheidung	divorce
sich scheiden lassen	to get divorced
der Scheidungsprozess	divorce proceedings
er ist geschieden	he is divorced
die hohe Scheidungsrate	high divorce rate
die Eheberatung	marriage guidance (counselling)
auf jn. eifersüchtig sein	to feel jealous of s.o.
sie passen nicht zusammen/ zueinander	they're incompatible
aufgrund der Unvereinbarkeit der Charaktere	on grounds of incompatibility
sie hat ein Kind aus erster Ehe	she has a child from her first marriage
ein außereheliches Kind	an illegitimate child
der/die Alleinerziehende	single parent
die alleinstehende Mutter	single mother
der alleinstehende Vater	single father
die meisten Geschiedenen heiraten erneut	most divorced people remarry
die Promiskuität	promiscuity
häufig den Partner wechseln	to be promiscuous
die Altersbeschwerden (pl)	infirmities of old age
in den Vorruhestand treten* (i-a-e)	to take early retirement

sich an den Ruhestand gewöhnen	to get used to being retired
die Rente	pension
der Seniorenpass (¨-e)	pensioner's bus/rail pass
die Witwe/der Witwer	widow/widower
die Beerdigung	funeral
um jn. trauern	to be in mourning for s.o.
zur Waise werden	to be orphaned
bis dass der Tod uns scheidet	till death us part

Die Schwangerschaft — Pregnancy

empfangen	to conceive
der Mutterschaftsurlaub	maternity leave
gebären (ie-a-o)	to give birth to
zur Welt kommen	to be born
sie bekommt ein Kind	she's having a baby
die Empfängnisverhütung	contraception
die (Antibaby-)Pille	contraceptive pill
das Kondom (-e)	condom
schwanger	pregnant
der Schwangerschaftstest	pregnancy test
eine (un-)erwünschte Schwangerschaft	a(n) (un)wanted pregnancy
der Fötus (pl Föten/Fötusse)	foetus
die Abtreibung / der Schwangerschaftsabbruch	abortion
ein Baby abtreiben lassen	to have an abortion
der Schutz des ungeborenen Lebens	the protection of the unborn child
die Fristenregelung	law allowing abortion within first 3 months
das Retortenbaby	test-tube baby
die künstliche Befruchtung	artificial insemination
jedes 6. Paar bleibt ungewollt kinderlos	one couple in 6 is unable to conceive
in gebärfähigem Alter	of child-bearing age

Die Familie — The family

die Kleinfamilie (-n)	small (nuclear) family
die Großfamilie (-n)	extended family
die Verwandtschaft	family (all relatives)
der Elternteil (sing)	parent

die Eltern (*pl*)	parents
der/die Erwachsene (*adj. noun*)	grown-up, adult
die Zwillinge (*pl*)	twins
der Schwager (⁻)	brother-in-law
die Schwägerin (-nen)	sister-in-law
die Schwiegereltern (*pl*)	in-laws
ein Kind erziehen	to bring up a child
Kinder großziehen	to raise a family
ein Baby stillen	to breast-feed a baby
die Kinderjahre (*pl*)	years of childhood
von Kind auf	from childhood
das gehört zu den Kindheitserinnerungen	that's part of one's childhood memories
im Kindesalter	at an early age
die Kindesmisshandlung	child abuse
der Pate/die Patin	godfather, godmother
taufen	to christen
die Konfirmation/Erstkommunion	confirmation/first communion
der/die Erziehungsberechtigte (*adj. noun*)	parent, legal guardian
das Kindermädchen (-)	nanny
die Tagesmutter	childminder
die leiblichen Eltern	natural parents
die Pflegeeltern	foster parents
das Pflegekind (-er)	foster child
die Stiefmutter/der Stiefvater	stepmother, -father
kindgemäß	suitable for children
der Buggy (-s)	pushchair, buggy
der Kinderfreibetrag	child allowance
die Schaffung emotionaler Geborgenheit	the creation of a sense of emotional security
das gefühlsmäßige Anklammern der Mutter an die Kinder	the mother's inability to let the children go emotionally
die Verantwortung für Entscheidungen teilen	to share responsibility for decisions
immer mehr Ehen bleiben kinderlos	more and more marriages remain childless
das liegt in der Familie	it runs in the family
streng	strict
autoritär	authoritarian
ein Kind verwöhnen	to spoil a child

15

die permissive Gesellschaft	permissive society
sie ist ein gut erzogenes Kind	she's a well brought up child
man soll Kinder zur Höflichkeit erziehen	children should be taught good manners
was für eine Beziehung hat er zu seinem Vater?	what sort of relationship does he have with his father?

F

Die Persönlichkeit

Character

I Positives

Positive aspects

jeder Mensch hat etwas ganz Besonderes	everyone has something special about them
einen guten Eindruck machen	to make a good impression
anpassungsfähig	adaptable
der Altruismus	altruism
treu/die Treue	faithful/ness, loyal/ty
kinderlieb	fond of children
großzügig/die Großzügigkeit	generous/generosity
ehrlich/die Ehrlichkeit	honest/y
selbständig/die Selbständigkeit	independent/independence
liebenswürdig/die Liebenswürdigkeit	kind/ness
er ist lebensfroh	he enjoys life
gehorsam/der Gehorsam	obedient, obedience
offen/die Offenheit	open/ness
bescheiden/die Bescheidenheit	modest/y
geduldig/die Geduld	patient/patience
unternehmungslustig	enterprising, adventurous
zuverlässig/die Zuverlässigkeit	reliable/reliability
zurückhaltend	reserved
verantwortungsbewusst	responsible
sparsam/die Sparsamkeit	thrifty/thriftiness
ruhig	calm
kontaktfreudig	outgoing
extravertiert	extrovert
gut angepasst	well-adjusted
lebhaft, temperamentvoll	lively, vivacious
der Ehrgeiz/ehrgeizig	ambition/ambitious
extravagant	flamboyant
idealistisch/der Idealismus	idealistic/idealism
vernünftig/die Vernunft	sensible/common sense

sensibel	sensitive
verständnisvoll	understanding
er hat Humor	he's got a good sense of humour

2 Negatives
Negative aspects

egoistisch	selfish
aggressiv	aggressive
arrogant/die Arroganz	arrogant, arrogance
brummig, grantig, mürrisch	cantankerous, grumpy
anstrengend	demanding
deprimiert/die Depression	depressed/depression
unehrlich/die Unehrlichkeit	dishonest/y
ungehorsam/der Ungehorsam	disobedient/disobedience
wankelmütig/die Wankelmütigkeit	fickle/ness
verklemmt	inhibited
die Hemmungen	inhibitions
er nimmt sich selbst zu ernst	he takes himself too seriously
verantwortungslos	irresponsible
reizbar	irritable
boshaft	malicious
geizig	mean (miserly)
gemein	mean (unkind)
egoistisch/der Egoismus	selfish/ness
angespannt	tense
verschlossen	withdrawn
schüchtern	shy
die Quatschtante / der Labermaul	chatterbox, tittle-tattler
unverschämt	outrageous, impudent
schmuddelig	sloppy
vulgär	vulgar
wahnsinnig	mad, crazy
unbeherrscht	lacking self-control
asozial	antisocial

Eltern und Teenager
Parents and teenagers

1 Teenager über Eltern
Teenagers on parents

sie hält ihre Eltern für	she considers her parents to be
– altmodisch	– old-fashioned
– verkalkt (*inf*), muffelig (*inf*)	– senile, fuddy-duddy, grumpy
– naiv	– naïve

– engstirnig	– narrow-minded
– heuchlerisch	– hypocritical
– wohlmeinend	– well-meaning
– streng	– strict
– verständnislos	– unsympathetic
– autoritär	– authoritarian
– voreingenommen (gegen)	– prejudiced (against)
sie hat geschimpft, weil ich ...	she told me off, because I ...
er geht mir auf die Nerven	he gets on my nerves
meine Eltern bestehen darauf, dass ...	my parents insist that ...
er kommt mit seinem Vater schlecht aus	he doesn't get on with his father
sie können sich in meine Lage versetzen	they can put themselves in my shoes
ich kann mit ihnen über nichts reden	I can't talk to them about anything
aufgeschlossen	open-minded
kompromissbereit	ready to compromise
sie verstehen sich gut	they get on well together
vorwurfsvoll	reproachful
strafen	to punish
ich komme nur schwer mit ... zurecht	I find it hard to cope with ...
sie nörgeln immer an mir herum	they're always nagging me
in den frühen Morgenstunden	in the small hours
kleinliche Vorschriften	petty rules
anständig	respectable
Respekt zeigen vor (+Dat)	to respect
man muss Respekt vor Älteren haben	you must respect your elders

2 Eltern über Teenager

Parents on teenagers

sie ist im Flegelalter	she's at that awkward adolescent stage
er ist total verdreht	he's all mixed up
deprimiert	depressed
die Emotionen, Empfindungen	feelings, emotions
lügen	to tell lies
unsicher	insecure
niedergeschlagen sein	to feel low

gleichgültig	indifferent
apathisch	apathetic
sich in seiner Haut nicht wohl fühlen	to feel ill at ease
die Clique	one's group of friends
alles in Frage stellen	to question everything
die Autorität in Frage stellen	to challenge authority
sie malt alles schwarzweiß	she paints everything black and white
in den Tag hinein leben	to live for the day
aus dem eigenen Schaden lernen	to learn the hard way
du willst das eine haben und das andere nicht lassen	you want it both ways
du nimmst deine Arbeit auf die leichte Schulter	you're not taking your work seriously enough
sich schlecht benehmen	to behave badly
fluchen	to use bad language, to swear
jn. beschimpfen	to swear at s.o.
das ist einzig und allein meine Sache	that's a matter for me alone
auf die schiefe Bahn geraten	to go off the rails
sich sonderbar kleiden	to dress outlandishly
sich über etw./jn. lustig machen	to make fun of sth./s.o.
kultiviert, fein	sophisticated, refined
gebildet	well-bred, educated
unmoralisch	immoral
ungezogen	ill-mannered
gute Manieren haben	to have good manners
lächerlich	ludicrous, ridiculous
die Verantwortung tragen	to take responsibility
die Markenklamotten	designer clothes

3 Der Konflikt — *Conflict*

minderjährig	under-age
Eltern haften für ihre Kinder	parents are responsible for their children
Rechte und Pflichten	rights and responsibilities
viel Wind um etw. machen	to make a fuss about sth.
viel Lärm um nichts	a storm in a teacup
ein wunder Punkt	a sore point
über etw. böse werden/sein	to get/be angry at sth.

auf jn. böse werden/sein	to get/be angry with s.o.
wütend reagieren	to react angrily
mir reißt die Geduld	my patience is wearing thin
die Beherrschung verlieren	to lose one's temper
sie reden nicht mehr miteinander	they're not talking to one another
sie haben sich gestritten	they've had a quarrel, argument
es gibt Krach wegen ...	there's trouble about ...
wir stimmen nicht überein	we don't agree
sie lässt sich von ihren Eltern nichts sagen	she won't be told anything by her parents
sie gehen in die Luft (*inf*)	they fly off the handle
es steht eine unsichtbare Wand zwischen mir und meinen Eltern	there's an invisible wall between me and my parents
ich bin nicht von gestern!	I wasn't born yesterday!
meckern	to moan, grumble
ärgern	to annoy
beleidigen	to insult
bei etw. (+*Dat*) ein Auge zudrücken	to turn a blind eye to sth.
das lasse ich mir nicht mehr gefallen	I won't put up with it any more
ich ziehe die Grenze bei (+*Dat*)	I draw the line at ...
sie geht mir auf die Nerven	she gets on my nerves
zugeben	to concede
jn. reizen	to provoke s.o.
seinen Willen durchsetzen	to get one's own way
ich nehme kein Blatt vor den Mund	I won't mince my words
ich falle mit der Tür ins Haus	I'll come straight to the point
wir besprechen Probleme gemeinsam	we talk problems over together
Ein Problem in einem offenen Gespräch lösen	to deal with a problem openly
lass uns offen reden	let's be open about this
sich wieder vertragen	to make it up
ausziehen*	to move out
das mache ich nicht mit!	I just won't stand for it!

www.bmfsfj.de
www.shell-jugend2000.de
www.jugendliche.de
www.jugendhilfe.net
www.youngnet.de
www.r-net.de/rheine/hnh/Projekt/start/

Die Gesundheit

3

Der gesunde Mensch

The healthy person

A

die präventive/kurative Medizin	preventative/curative medicine
vorbeugen ist besser als heilen	prevention is better than cure
das Gesundheitswesen	Health Service
die Krankenversicherung	health insurance
die Körperpflege	personal hygiene
sich fit halten	to keep fit
kerngesund sein	to be as fit as a fiddle
er bekommt nicht genug Bewegung	he doesn't get enough exercise
das gesunde Essen	healthy diet
die Frischkost	fresh food
lebensnotwendig	essential
Ballaststoffe (pl)	fibre (in the diet)
eine Kur machen	to go on a health cure
der Kurort (-e)	health resort
der Fitness-Club	health club
abnehmen/zunehmen	to lose/put on weight
eine Schlankheitskur machen	to go on a diet
sich wohl/nicht wohl fühlen	to feel well/ill
die Periode (-n)	period
die Menstruationsbeschwerden (pl)	period pains
die Frauenklinik (-en)	well-woman clinic

Körperliche Krankheiten

Physical illnesses

B

eine Untersuchung machen lassen	to go for a medical examination
entdecken	to bring to light, detect
behandeln	to treat
heilen	to cure
sich erholen	to recover
nicht ganz auf der Höhe	a bit under the weather
der Virus (pl Viren)/der Erreger (-)	virus
der Keim (-e)	germ
sie hat eine Allergie gegen (+Acc)	she's allergic to
die Epidemie (-n)	epidemic
ansteckend	infectious, contagious
die Tropenkrankheit (-en)	tropical disease
sich ... holen	to catch ...

sich erkälten	to catch cold
krank werden, erkranken	to fall ill
leiden (ei-litt-gelitten) an (+Dat)	to suffer from
schmerzhaft	painful
verunglücken	to have an accident
bei einem Unfall verletzt	injured in an accident
die Wunde (-n)	wound
ohnmächtig werden	to faint
der (Körper-)Behinderte (adj. noun)	(physically) disabled person
blind	blind
taub	deaf
stumm	dumb

Die medizinische Behandlung	**Medical treatment**
der/die praktische Arzt/Ärztin	general practitioner
der/die Facharzt/ärztin	specialist
der Chirurg (-en)	surgeon
die Krankenschwester (-n)	nurse
der Krankenpfleger (-)	(male) nurse
die Hebamme (-n)	midwife
einen Arzt holen	to call a doctor
Schmerzen (pl) lindern	to relieve pain
verschreiben	to prescribe
ein Medikament verschrieben bekommen	to be prescribed a drug
das Rezept (-e)	prescription
die Tablette (-n)	pill, tablet
die Dosis	dose
die Medikamente (pl) } die Arzneimittel (pl) }	medication, drugs
das Schmerzmittel (-)	pain-killer, analgesic
die Nebenwirkungen (pl)	side effects
die Schutzimpfung (-en)	vaccination
geimpft werden	to have a vaccination
jn. beatmen	to give s.o. artificial respiration
röntgen	to X-ray
operiert werden	to have an operation
die Vollnarkose	general anaesthetic
die örtliche Betäubung	local anaesthetic
narkotisieren	to anaesthetise
die Verpflanzung	transplant

der Operationssaal (-säle)	operating theatre
die Blutübertragung (-en)	blood transfusion
jm. strenge Bettruhe verordnen	to confine s.o. to bed
der Rollstuhl (-̈e)	wheelchair
die Intensivstation	intensive care unit

Der Altersprozess — The aging process

alt werden	to age
nachlassende Kräfte	failing powers
im Vollbesitz seiner geistigen Kräfte	in full possession of one's mental faculties
rüstig	spritely
Kreislaufstörungen (pl)	circulation/heart disorders
die Herzkrankheit	heart disease
herzkrank sein	to have a heart complaint
an einem Herzinfarkt sterben	to die of a heart attack
der Krebs	cancer
die Strahlentherapie	radiotherapy
bösartig, gutartig	malignant, benign
der Bluthochdruck	high blood pressure
Krebs erregend	carcinogenic
die Todesrate unter (+Dat) ...	the death rate among ...
die Lebenserwartung	life expectancy
dem Kranken ist nicht mehr zu helfen	the patient is beyond help
unheilbar	terminally ill
den Hirntod feststellen	to establish that s.o. is brain dead
die Sterbehilfe	euthanasia
jn. künstlich am Leben erhalten	to keep s.o. alive artificially
jm. zum Selbstmord verhelfen	to help s.o. to commit suicide
das Leiden unnötig verlängern	to prolong suffering unnecessarily
um das Leben kämpfen	to fight to keep s.o. alive
der menschenwürdige Lebensabschluss	a humane end to one's life
die Grauzone (-n)	grey area (of law, morality)

Psychische Probleme — Psychological problems

im Stress (masc) sein	to be stressed
an Schlaflosigkeit leiden (ei-i-i)	to suffer from insomnia
geisteskrank	mentally ill

psychisch gestört	emotionally disturbed
die Depression (-en)	depression
deprimiert sein	to be depressed
die Magersucht	anorexia
der/die Psychiater/in	psychiatrist
die Nerven (*pl*)	nerves
Beruhigungsmittel nehmen	to take tranquillisers
mit den Nerven völlig am Ende sein	to be a nervous wreck
einen Nervenzusammenbruch erleiden (ei-i-i)	to have a nervous breakdown
das Leben nicht verkraften können	to feel unable to face life
Selbstmord begehen	to commit suicide
ausweglos	hopeless
verzweifelt sein	to feel desperate
die Telefonseelsorge	the Samaritans

F

Das Rauchen	**Smoking**
der Nichtraucher (-)	non-smoker
inhalieren	to inhale
paffen (*inf*)	to puff
der Kettenraucher	chain-smoker
außer Atem kommen	to get out of breath
der Raucherhusten	smoker's cough
das Passivrauchen	passive smoking
der Qualm	thick smoke, fog
das Nikotin	nicotine
nikotingelb	nicotine stained
er/sie stinkt nach Rauch	he/she smells of smoke
die Suchtkrankheit	addiction
vom Rauchen vergilbte Zähne	teeth stained yellow by smoking
der Teer	tar
die Lunge (-n)	lung
an Lungenkrebs sterben	to die of lung cancer
seine Gesundheit schädigen	to damage one's health
asozial	antisocial
seine Unsicherheit überspielen	to hide one's insecurity
sich (*Dat*) das Rauchen abgewöhnen	to give up smoking
die Werbung einschränken	to restrict advertising
eine Todesursache, die man vermeiden kann	an avoidable cause of death

Der Alkoholkonsum

seinen Kummer mit Alkohol betäuben	to drown one's sorrows with alcohol
die Reflexe lassen nach	one's reflexes slow down
seine Hemmungen verlieren	to lose one's inhibitions
sich betrinken	to get drunk
besoffen (inf.), betrunken	drunk
nüchtern	sober
blau wie ein Veilchen	drunk as a lord
die Trunksucht	alcoholism
Alkoholiker sein	to be an alcoholic
der Kater	hangover
noch eins zum Abgewöhnen	one for the road
die Trunkenheit am Steuer	drink driving
einen Unfall verursachen	to cause an accident
ins Röhrchen blasen	to take a breath test
der Blutalkoholspiegel	blood-alcohol level
die Promillegrenze	the legal alcohol limit
die Anhebung der Alkoholsteuer	raising the tax on alcohol
die Aufklärung	education campaign
die Sauftour/der Kneipenbummel	pub crawl

Alcohol consumption

AIDS

das menschliche Abwehrsystem	the human immune system
zusammenbrechen	to break down
durch Blut übertragen	to transmit by blood
die Zeit von der Ansteckung bis zum Auftreten der Krankheit	the time from infection to the appearance of the disease
sich mit Aids infizieren	to catch Aids
an AIDS erkrankt	ill with AIDS
der/die Infizierte	infected person
sich verbreiten (itr)	to spread
der/die Betroffene	affected person
am schwersten betroffen sind ...	worst affected are ...
der/die Homosexuelle (adj. noun)	homosexual, lesbian
der Bluter	haemophiliac
der Geschlechtsverkehr	sexual intercourse
die Immunschwäche	immune deficiency

AIDS

Die Drogen

Drugs

die Droge (-n) das Rauschgift (-e) }	drugs (addictive)
die Flucht	a means of escape
im Rausch	under the influence of drink/drugs
das Einnehmen von Drogen	the consumption of drugs
der Drogenmissbrauch	drug abuse
die Wirkung (-en)	effect
stumpfsinnig	humdrum, monotonous
aussteigen	to drop out
aus Neugierde	from curiosity
eine weiche Droge	soft drug
der Cannabis, das ‚Gras', Haschisch	cannabis, 'pot'
auf harte Drogen umsteigen	to move on to hard drugs
das Kokain, das Heroin	cocaine, heroin
sich (etw.) spritzen	to inject o.s. (with sth.)
schnüffeln	to sniff (drugs)
Euphoriegefühle erzeugen	to produce feelings of euphoria
der Dealer, Pusher	dealer, pusher
der Rauschgifthandel	drugs trafficking
beschlagnahmen	to confiscate
legalisieren	to legalise
heroinsüchtig werden	to become addicted to heroin
zur Abhängigkeit führen	to cause addiction
der Rauschgiftsüchtige (*adj. noun*) der Drogenabhängige (*adj. noun*) }	drug addict
eine tödliche Dosis	a fatal dose
die Wiedereingliederung	rehabilitation
das Rehabilitationszentrum (*pl* -zentren)	rehabilitation centre
vom Kokain runterkommen (*inf*)	to kick cocaine
aufgeben	to give up
die Entziehungskur	cure for addiction
die Entzugserscheinungen (*pl*)	withdrawal symptoms
zittern	to shake, shiver
rückfällig werden	to go back (onto drugs)

www.BMGesundheit.de	www.sport.de
www.dge.de	www.sucht.de

Die Medien

4

Der Rundfunk

I Die Technik

der Hörfunk
das Fernsehen
der Fernsehapparat }
der Fernseher }
die Glotze (inf)
der Bildschirm (-e)
einschalten, ausschalten
umschalten
zappen
die Fernsteuerung
der Videorekorder (-)
aufzeichnen, aufnehmen
die Aufnahme (-n)
die bespielte Kassette (-n)
der Video-/Bildschirmtext
das Satellitenfernsehen
die Parabolantenne (-n)
empfangen
das Kabelfernsehen
über Kabel übertragen
digitales Fernsehen
der Sender (-)
der Kanal (-̈e)
das Programm (-e)
ausstrahlen
die Sendung (-en)
auf regionaler Ebene
die Lokalradiostation (-en)

2 Die Programmgestaltung

der Zuschauer (-)
der Zuhörer (-)
unterhalten (insep)
was kommt heute abend im
   Fernsehen?

Broadcasting

Technology

radio
television (the medium)
television (set)

goggle box
screen
to switch on, to switch off
to change channels
to flick from one channel to another
remote control
video recorder
to record
recording
pre-recorded cassette
teletext
satellite television
satellite dish
to record
cable television
to transmit by cable
digital television
station
channel
channel, programme guide
to broadcast
broadcast, programme
on a regional level
local radio station

Programme planning

viewer (*pl:* also audience)
listener (*pl:* also audience)
to entertain
what's on television this evening?

die Unterhaltungssendung (-en)	light entertainment programme
die Fernsehserie (-n)	soap opera
die Dokumentarsendung (-en)	documentary
das Schulfernsehen	broadcasting for schools
der Spielfilm (-e)	feature film
der Zeichentrickfilm (-e)	cartoon
synchronisiert	dubbed
mit Untertiteln	with subtitles
die aktuelle Sendung	current affairs programme
die Nachrichtensendung (-en) ⎫ die Tagesschau ⎭	news
‚Sie hören Nachrichten‘	'Here is the news' (radio)
der Nachrichtensprecher (-)	newsreader
der Ansager (-)	announcer
der Moderator	presenter
der Überblick	summary
die Verkehrsmeldung (-en)	traffic report
uralt	ancient
die Wiederholung (-en)	repeat
zum x-ten Mal	for the n-th time
Live-Sendungen lassen den Zuschauer am aktuellen Geschehen teilhaben	live broadcasts allow the viewer to keep up with events as they happen
Lehr-	educational
Kultur-	cultural
vorführen	to show
ein erweitertes Angebot von Sendungen	a greater range of programmes
die Vielfalt	great variety
Die Zuschauerzahlen (pl) ⎫ die Einschaltquote ⎭	viewing figures
der Werbespot (-s)	advertisement
der Werbeblock (¨e)	commercial break
sich durch Werbeeinnahmen finanzieren	to be financed by advertising revenue

3 Probleme

Problems

sie verherrlichen die Gewalt	they glorify violence
eine über die Medien transportierte Tolerierung der Gewalt	a tolerance of violence conveyed by the media
gewaltsam	violent

verharmlosen	to make sth. appear harmless
die Brutalität	brutality
die Schießerei	shooting/shootout
der Horrorfilm (-e)	horror-film/video nasty
die Videothek (-en)	video shop/library
die Pornographie	pornography
es steht im Mittelpunkt pädagogischer Kritik	it is at the centre of criticism from educationists
die heile Familie	secure, normal family
hier wird keine heile Welt vorgeführt	there's no utopia shown here
die Scheinwelt	a bogus world
der Verlust von Phantasie	loss of one's imagination
sie klebt am Fernseher	she's glued to the set
die Auswirkung auf das Verhalten	the effect on behaviour
es lässt dich verdummen	it dulls your mind
sie wenden viel zu viel Zeit für Fernsehen auf	they spend far too much time watching television
Eltern sollten verhindern, dass Kinder ...	parents should prevent their children from ...
sie beschäftigen sich zu wenig mit ihren Kindern	they take too little interest in their children
eine Alternative bieten	to offer an alternative
kreative Tätigkeiten (pl)	creative activities
es beeinflusst unsere Wertvorstellungen	it influences our moral values
Besteht ein direkter Zusammenhang zwischen Gewaltdarstellungen und Jugendkriminalität?	Is there a direct link between the depiction of violence and teenage crime?
wertlos	worthless
passiv	passive
die unkritische Haltung	uncritical attitude
vertrotteln (inf), vegetieren	to vegetate
beeinflussen	to influence
verbreiten	to disseminate
trivial	trivial

Die Presse

The press

B

I Die Tageszeitungen

Daily papers

die überregionale Zeitung (-en)	national newspaper

die Illustrierte (-n) ⎱ die Zeitschrift (-en) ⎰	magazine
das Fachblatt (¨er)	specialist magazine
das Anzeigenblatt (¨er)	local advertising paper
erscheinen	to be published
eine Zeitung herausgeben	to publish a newspaper
der Verlag (-e)	publishing company
monatlich	monthly
wöchentlich	weekly
das Comic-Heft (-e)	comic
der/die Leser/in	reader
die Leserschaft	readership
abonnieren	to subscribe to
das Jahresabonnement	a year's subscription
der Abonnent (-en)	subscriber
durchblättern (insep)	to flick through
der Zeitungshändler (-)	newsagent
die Auflage	circulation
auflagenstark	with a big circulation
die Ausgabe (-n)	edition
das Käseblatt (¨e) (inf)	local rag (inf)
die Ortszeitung (-en)	local paper
die Boulevardpresse	gutter press
die Boulevardzeitung (-en)	tabloid paper
die Regenbogenpresse	trash magazines

2 Die Redaktion — *Editing*

der/die Redakteur/in	editor
die Redaktion	editorial staff
Briefe an die Herausgeber	letters to the editor
nach Redaktionsschluss eingegangen	'stop press'
die Schlagzeile (-n)	headline
die Aufmachung	presentation, layout
die Balkenüberschrift (-en)	banner headline
der Leitartikel (-)	leading article
der Kommentar	comment, analysis
etw. kommentieren	to comment on sth.
aktuelle Ereignisse	current events
der Reporter (-)	reporter
der Journalist (-en)	journalist

der Augenzeuge/-zeugin	eye witness
berichten über (+Acc) ⎫ melden ⎭	to report
die Nachricht (-en)	items of news
der Bericht (-e), die Meldung (-en)	report
die Reportage	(longer, fuller) report
die Sportseite (-n)	sports page
die Kolumne (-n)	column (article & page division)
die Lokalnachrichten (pl)	local news
die Berichterstattung	reporting
die Kurznachrichten (pl)	short news items
das Feuilleton (-s)	feature/review section
Leserbriefe	readers' letters
das Farbmagazin (-e)	colour supplement
die Presseagentur (-en)	press agency
‚Veranstaltungen‘	'What's On'
das Inserat (-e)	small ad
das Werbung, die Reklame	advertising
der Nachruf (-e)	obituary
die Kritik (-en)	critique, critical review
der Kritiker (-)	critic
die Klatschspalte (-n)	gossip column
die Problemseite (-n) ⎫ der Kummerkasten (⏜) ⎭	problem page
das Ereignis (-se)	event
sich ereignen ⎫ geschehen (ie-a-e)* ⎪ vorgehen* ⎬ sich abspielen ⎭	to take place
sich/einen auf dem Laufenden halten	to keep o.s./s.o. up to date
von aktuellem Interesse	of current interest
richtunggebend	influential
voreingenommen	biased
etw. einseitig schildern	to report sth. in a biased way
reißerisch	sensational
die Enthüllungen (pl)	revelations
unsachlich, subjektiv	subjective
sachlich, objektiv	objective
ausführlich	full, detailed
informativ	informative

ein Zerrbild entwerfen	to give a distorted picture
der Knüller	scoop
sie greifen (ei-i-i) in die Privatsphäre ein	they invade people's privacy
die Pressefreiheit	freedom of the press
seine Macht missbrauchen	to abuse one's power
eine Zeitung auf Schadenersatz verklagen	to claim damages from a newspaper
die Verleumdung	libel
die Pressezensur	censorship
die Pressekonzentration	ownership of the press by a few
Es bildet eine Gefahr für die Meinungsvielfalt dar	It threatens to restrict the expression of a variety of opinions

C ## Die Werbung — **Advertising**

die Konsumgesellschaft	consumer society
die Werbewirtschaft	advertising industry
die Werbeausgaben (pl)	expenditure on advertising
der Werbeslogan (-s)	advertising slogan
der Werbegag (-s)	stunt
die Werbekampagne (-n) } die Werbeaktion (-en) }	advertising campaign
die Werbeagentur (-en)	advertising agency
das Werbefernsehen (-)	television advertising
die Kleinanzeige (-n)	small ad
werbewirksam sein	to have good publicity value
sein Image verbessern	to improve one's image
die Marktforschung	market research
Waren mit erstrebenswerten Eigenschaften verknüpfen	to link a product to desirable qualities
Prominente werden eingesetzt	well-known people are used
einem Produkt Prestige verleihen (ei-ie-ie)	to give a product some prestige
die Plakatwand (¨e)	hoarding/billboard
werben (i-a-o) für	to promote
ein Produkt auf den Markt bringen	to bring out a product
die Zielgruppe (-n)	target group
überzeugend	persuasive
verführen	to tempt
überreden	to persuade

überzeugen	to convince
die Werbeaussage	advertising message
als Blickfang	to catch the eye
etw. ansprechen	to appeal to sth.
die niederen Instinkte	our baser instincts
ausnutzen	to take advantage of
ausbeuten	to exploit, use
zum Kauf animieren	to motivate people to buy
der Lebensstil	life-style
der Konsument (*weak noun*) der Verbraucher (-)	consumer
der Konsumterror	pressures of consumer society
der Konsumzwang	pressure to buy unnecessary goods
die Kauflust	desire to buy things
den Markt sättigen	to saturate the market
der Markt ist hart umkämpft	there is strong competition
die Aufmerksamkeit auf ein Produkt lenken	to draw attention to a product
sie erfüllen alle dieselbe Funktion	they all do the same thing
unbewusst	subconscious
einen positiven Eindruck erwecken	to give a favourable impression
Erwartungen prägen	to shape expectations
Ansprüche, die nicht zu erfüllen sind	demands which cannot be met
Konsumbedürfnisse wecken	to create needs
über seine Verhältnisse leben	to live beyond one's means
sich ein Statussymbol anschaffen	to acquire/purchase a status symbol
die Kaufkraft der Jugendlichen	the purchasing power of young people

www.virtourist.com/newspapers/europe.htm
www.werbung.at
www.welt.de
www.bild.de
www.derstandard.at

Schule und Ausbildung

5

A Das Schulsystem / Education system

die allgemeine Schulpflichtzeit	(period of) compulsory schooling
der Kindergarten (¨)	kindergarten, nursery school
die Grundschule (-n)	primary school
das Gymnasium (pl Gymnasien)	grammar school (11–19)
die Realschule (-n)	secondary/technical school (11–16)
die Hauptschule (-n)	secondary modern school (11–15)
die Gesamtschule (-n)	comprehensive school
die Privatschule (-n)	private school
das Internat (-e)	boarding school
das Abitur (no pl)	'A' levels, Higher Grades
der Realschulabschluss / der Hauptschulabschluss	secondary school leaving certificate
die Orientierungsstufe	first 2 years of secondary education
die Schule besuchen	to go to school
sitzen bleiben	to repeat a year
er wurde nicht versetzt	he has had to repeat a year
die Oberstufe	last 3 years of Gymnasium
der Lehrplan/Bildungsplan	curriculum
die Fächerauswahl	choice of subjects
das Wahlfach (¨er)	optional subject
die Kernfächer (pl)	basic/core subjects
die Pflichtfächer (pl)	compulsory subjects
das Leistungsfach (¨er)	main 'A' level subject
die Nachhilfestunde (-n)	extra tuition
Lesen, Schreiben und Rechnen	the 3 Rs
der Elternabend	parents' evening

B Die Prüfungen / Examinations

der Abiturient (-en)	student in last year of Gymnasium
mündlich, schriftlich	oral, written
die Klausur	piece of work done under exam conditions
die kontinuierliche Beurteilung	continuous assessment
die Klassenarbeit (-en)	class test (for continuous assessment)
gute Noten bekommen	to get good marks/grades

die Endnote	final mark
das Zeugnis (-se)	report
eine Prüfung machen	to sit for an exam
eine Prüfung bestehen (*irreg*)	to pass an exam
durchfallen	to fail an exam
er ist in Mathe durchgefallen	he failed in Maths
er ist durchgerutscht	he scraped through
eine Prüfung wiederholen	to retake/resit an exam
sich auf seine Prüfungen vorbereiten	to prepare for the exams
eine Konkurrenzatmosphäre	a competitive atmosphere
leistungsorientiert	competitive (person, school)
der Leistungsdruck	pressure to achieve

Die Schüler

Pupils

1 Der Lernprozess

The learning process

die Aufmerksamkeit	attentiveness
das Gedächtnis die Gedächtniskraft }	memory
ein fotografisches Gedächtnis	photographic memory
die Gedächtnishilfe	memory aid
ohne Fleiß kein Preis	no pain, no gain (*proverb*)
das Arbeitstier (-e)	workaholic
der Streber (-)	swot

ich brauche immer eine
  Geräuschkulisse
	I always need some background
	  noise

stichwortartige Notizen	outline notes
wiederholen	to revise
pauken (*inf*)	to cram
sich überarbeiten (*insep*)	to overwork
die Legasthenie/der Legastheniker	dyslexia/dyslexic person
lernbehindert	educationally handicapped

2 Positive Einstellung

Positive attitude

ich bin sehr motiviert	I'm well motivated
ein begabter Schüler	a gifted pupil
ich bin gut in Englisch	I'm good at English
etw. auswendig lernen	to learn sth. by heart
die Wissenslücken stopfen	to fill in the gaps
der Wissensdurst	thirst for knowledge

sich Wissen zulegen	to acquire knowledge
sich auf dem Laufenden halten	to keep o.s. up to date
begreifen (ei-i-i)	to grasp
sich sehr bemühen, etw. zu tun	to make every effort to do sth.
es kostet große Mühe	it's a real effort
sein Bestes tun	to do one's best
arbeiten, so gut man kann	to work to the best of one's ability
ich beherrsche das Wesentliche	I have a good grasp of the basics
sie ist den anderen haushoch überlegen	she's way ahead of the others
das Ehrgeiz; ehrgeizig	ambition; ambitious

3 Negative Einstellung

Negative attitude

das geht über meinen Verstand	that's beyond me
ich lerne nur auf äußeren Druck	I only learn when forced to
es fehlt mir an Konzentration	I lack concentration
die Anstrengung lohnt sich nicht	it's not worth the effort
ich bin für Mathe nicht begabt	I'm not very good at Maths
Ich drücke mich um die Hausaufgaben	I make excuses to get out of doing my homework
durchwursteln (*inf*)	to muddle through
das begreife ich einfach nicht	I just don't get it
ich muss mir den Kopf zerbrechen	I have to rack my brains
einen Aufsatz hinrotzen	to dash off an essay
mit seiner Arbeit im Rückstand sein*	to be behind with one's work
die Schule schwänzen	to play truant
abschreiben	to copy
bei einer Prüfung mogeln/pfuschen	to cheat in an exam
jn. schickanieren	to bully s.o.
verprügeln	to beat up

D

Die Lehrer

Teachers

sich um ein Lehramt bewerben (i-a-o)	to apply for a teaching job
der Schuldirektor (-en)	head teacher
der Studienreferendar (-e)	probationary teacher
Schüler/ein Fach unterrichten	to teach pupils/a subject
das Kollegium	teaching staff
die Lehrerkonferenz (-en)	staff meeting
der Lernstoff	material to be learned
abwechslungsreich	varied

wir befassen uns mit ...	we're dealing with ...
korrigieren	to mark
gerecht, fair	fair
jeden gleich behandeln	to treat everyone the same
die Kluft zwischen Theorie und Praxis	the gap between theory and practice
er stellt hohe Ansprüche	he sets high standards
ein gutes Lernklima	a good atmosphere for study
konsquent	consistent
sie fesselt unser Interesse	she engages our interest
er macht einen guten Unterricht	he teaches well
schwafeln (inf)	to waffle
lasch	lax
locker	laid-back
sich durchsetzen	to be assertive
unnahbar	distant, unapproachable
eine Beziehung zu seinen Schülern finden	to relate to one's pupils
die Disziplin aufrechterhalten	to maintain discipline
die Disziplin straffen	to tighten up discipline
motivieren	to motivate
Diskussionen fördern	to encourage discussion
bestrafen	to punish
einen Schüler eine Stunde nachsitzen lassen	to give a pupil an hour's detention
sie sitzt nach	she's in detention

Die Ausbildung

Training

E

die Berufsschule (-n)	training/F.E. college
der Ausbildungsplatz (:-e)	position for trainee
der Auszubildende (adj. noun) der Azubi (-s)	trainee
die Lehre (-n)/der Lehrling (-e)	apprenticeship, training/apprentice
die kaufmännische Ausbildung	business management training
sich weiterbilden	to continue one's education/training
berufsorientiert	work-orientated
die Einarbeitung	introductory training in company
das Ausbildungsprogramm	training scheme
der Mangel an Ausbildungsplätzen	lack of traineeships
man sollte mehr Ausbildungsplätze zur Verfügung stellen	more training places should be made available

ein Versager sein*	to be a failure (at school)
der zweite Bildungsweg	means of improving qualifications through night school, etc.
die Volkshochschule (-n)	adult education school
das Abitur nachholen	to take A-levels later on
die Abendschule	evening class, night school

F

Die Bildungspolitik | **Educational policy**

die beherrschenden Themen der Bildungsdebatte	the main topics in the debate about education
die elternlichen Erwartungen erfüllen	to fulfil parental expectations
der Etat für Schulen	state expenditure on schools
das Schul- u. Wissenschafts-ministerium	ministry of education
die Lernmittelfreiheit	free choice of teaching materials
sie haben die Wahl zwischen mehreren Möglichkeiten	they have the choice of several possibilities
je nach Neigungen und Fähigkeiten	according to interests and abilities
Reformen durchführen	to carry out reforms
das hat zur Folge gehabt, dass ...	the result of this has been that ...
es muss vorrangig behandelt werden	it must be given top priority
oben/unten auf der Prioritätenliste	high/low on the list of priorities
gut ausgestattet	well-equipped
am Arbeitsmarkt orientiert	orientated towards the job market
sinkende Schülerzahlen	falling numbers of pupils
überfüllte Klassen	overcrowded classes
die Klassenstärke senken	to reduce class sizes
gravierende Leistungsmängel (pl)	serious underachievement
sie laden ihre Aggression in der Schule ab	they vent their aggression in school
leistungsstarke Schüler sollen verstärkt gefördert werden	able pupils should be stretched
das nachlassende Leistungsniveau	falling standards (of achievement)
den Leistungsstand beurteilen	to assess achievement
die Leistungen steigern	to raise standards
eine falsche (Selbst-)Einschätzung des Leistungsvermögens	a false assessment of (one's own) abilities
den Leistungswettbewerb verstärken	to make things more competitive

Schüler zu geistiger Selbständigkeit erziehen (ie-o-o) — to educate pupils to think for themselves

Die Sonderschule

Special school

man nimmt auf ihre Behinderungen Rücksicht — they take account of their disabilities

man fördert die vorhandenen Fähigkeiten — they build on the abilities they have

Ausbildungschancen versäumen — to miss out on educational opportunities

die Chancengleichheit — equality of opportunity

die Blindenschrift — braille

die Zeichensprache — sign language

Das Hochschulsystem

Higher education

die Schule verlassen — to leave school

studieren — to continue one's studies

auf die Universität gehen ⎫
die Universität besuchen ⎭ — to go to university

die Fachhochschule — tertiary technical college

die Universität Bonn — University of Bonn

die Geisteswissenschaften (*pl*) — humanities

die Naturwissenschaften (*pl*) — sciences

die Hochschulerziehung — higher education

das Abitur berechtigt zum Studium an der Universität — A-levels give you the right to study at university

der Numerus Clausus — restricted entry quota to university

der Studienplatz — place at university

sich um einen Studienplatz bewerben — to apply for a place at university

das Auswahlgespräch (-e) — interview

das Universitätsgelände (-) — campus

die Mensa — students' refectory, canteen

das Studentenwohnheim (-e) — hall of residence, hostel

die Studentenbude (-n) — student digs, bedsit

ich studiere Mathe — I'm doing a Maths degree

einen akademischen Grad erhalten (ä-ie-a) — to get a degree

dazu ist ein Universitätsstudium erforderlich — a degree is required for that

promovieren	to do a doctorate, doctoral thesis
nach Abschluss des Studiums	after qualifying
die gegenseitige Anerkennung von Hochschuldiplomen	mutual recognition of university degrees (in EU countries)
er kriegt BAföG	he gets a grant
die Studiengebühren	tuition fees
das Studium abbrechen	to drop out of one's course
ein Studium finanzieren	to finance a course of study
für Härtefälle (*pl*)	in cases of hardship
das Darlehen	loan
seinen Horizont erweitern	to broaden one's mind
sie hat Esprit	she's got a good brain
ein Fach intensiv studieren	to study a subject in depth
der Hochschulabsolvent (-en) (*weak noun*)	graduate
Forschung betreiben (ei-ie-ie)	to do research

www.abitur.de
www.san-ev.de
www.studieren.de

Eine Stelle suchen

Looking for a job

A

der Beruf (-e)
career

der/die Berufsberater/in
careers adviser

die Berufswahl
choice of career

ich möchte einen Beruf in
Richtung Elektronik ergreifen
I'd like to go for a career that has
something to do with electronics

im Sprachenbereich
in the field of languages

eine passende Stelle
a suitable job

eine freie Stelle
vacancy

den Anzeigenteil der Zeitung
ansehen
to look at the advertisements in the
newspaper

die Annonce (-n)
advertisement

einstellen
to employ

die Stellenangebote (pl)
situations vacant

welche Anforderungen werden an
Ausbildung gestellt?
what are the requirements in terms
of training?

sich in (+Dat) ... auskennen
müssen
to have to know about ...

unterqualifiziert sein
to be under-qualified

die Eigenschaft (-en)
(personal) characteristic

das Arbeitsamt
job centre

die Stellenvermittlung (-en)
employment agency

die Branche (-n)
area of business, trade, industry

die Abteilung (-en)
department (of company)

die Arbeitsmarktlage
state of the job market

das erfordert Ihre Eigeninitiative
you have to use your own initiative

eine Firma direkt anschreiben
to write to a firm direct

ein begehrter Posten
a much sought-after job

jn. um Rat fragen
to ask s.o. for advice

Die Bewerbung

Application

B

das Bewerbungsformular (-e)
application form

sich bei einer Firma um eine Stelle
bewerben
to apply to a company for a job

das Bewerbungsschreiben (-)
letter (of application)

der Lebenslauf
curriculum vitæ, c.v.

das Foto (-s) ⎱ das Lichtbild (-er) ⎰	photograph
persönliche Daten (*pl*)	personal details
die Qualifikationen (*pl*)	qualifications
die Berufserfahrung	experience (professional)
gute Kenntnisse in ...	a good knowledge of ...
Deutschkenntnisse erforderlich	a knowledge of German required
seine EDV-Kenntnisse ausnutzen	to use one's knowledge of computers
die Fotokopie (-n)	photocopy
die Unterlagen (*pl*)	documents
etw. beilegen	to enclose sth. (with a letter)
jn. als Referenz angeben	to give s.o. as a referee

Das Vorstellungsgespräch

Interview

jn. zum Vorstellungsgespräch einladen	to invite s.o. for interview
der Gesprächspartner (-)	interviewer
dezente Kleidung tragen	to dress well
gepflegt	well-groomed
wie verhalten Sie sich in einer Stress-Situation?	how do you react in stressful situations?
Testverfahren einsetzen	to use tests
man will damit ermitteln, ob ein Bewerber der Stelle gewachsen ist	they want to use them to find out whether an applicant is suitable for the job
ist der Test ausschlaggebend?	is the test decisive?
Geschick im Umgang mit Menschen haben ⎱ geschickt mit Menschen umgehen können ⎰	to be good at dealing with people
gute Umgangsformen	good manners
Sie bekommen einen schriftlichen Bescheid	you will receive notification in writing
jm. eine Absage erteilen	to turn s.o. down
man hat mir die Stelle angeboten	they offered me the job
die Zusage (-n)	(firm) job offer
die Aufgabe (-n)	task
wie sehen die Aufstiegs- möglichkeiten aus?	what are the career prospects?
es ist ein Schritt nach vorn	it's a step up the ladder

sich hocharbeiten	to work one's way up
die Verdienstmöglichkeiten	earnings potential
der Arbeitsvertrag (¨e)	job contract
der gesicherte Arbeitsplatz (¨e)	job security

Die Arbeit

Employment

D

I Die Arbeitswelt

The world of work

der Arbeitgeber (-)	employer
der ständige Konkurrenzkampf	rat race
pendeln/der Pendler (-)	to commute/commuter
die Hauptverkehrszeit	rush hour
auf dem Weg nach oben sein	to be on the way up
befördert werden	to gain promotion
durch Erfahrung lernen	to learn by experience
in eine leitende Stellung aufrücken	to reach a top position
im Aufsichtsrat sitzen	to be on the board of directors
der Aufsichtsratsvorsitzende (*adj. noun*)	chairman of the board
die Mitbestimmung	co-determination/worker participation in management
der Betriebsleiter (-)	works manager
der Personalleiter (-)	personnel manager
der Verkaufsleiter (-)	sales manager
der Vorarbeiter (-) der Vorgesetzte (*adj. noun*)	foreman
der Kollege (-n) der Mitarbeiter (-)	colleague
die Stellung (-en)	job, position
beschäftigen	to employ
der/die Arbeitnehmer/in (-/nen)	employee
die Belegschaft	workforce (of company)
die Arbeitskräfte (*pl*)	workforce, manpower
die Erwerbstätigen (*pl*)	the working population
berufstätig	working, having a job
beschäftigt	busy (a lot to do)
belebt, geschäftig	busy (lively)
leistungsorientiert arbeiten	to aim for efficiency
der steigende Leistungsdruck	increasing pressure to do well
das Mobbing	bullying/harrassment
sie arbeitet bei Daimler-Benz	she works for Daimler-Benz

schwarz arbeiten	to work illegally
die Abwesenheitsquote	the rate of absenteeism
das Gewerbe (-)	trade
das Baugewerbe	construction industry
das Hotelgewerbe	hotel trade
der öffentliche Dienst	civil service
der Beamte (*adj. noun*) ⎱ die Beamtin ⎰	civil servant
die Dienstleistungen (*pl*)	service industries
das Bankwesen	banking
die Publicrelations/Public Relations	Public Relations
die Werbeagentur (-en)	advertising agency
der Verlag (-e)	publishing company
die Reiseagentur (-en)	travel agent
der Buchhalter (-)	accountant
die Abteilung (-en)	department
die Zentrale (-n) ⎱ die Hauptstelle (-n) ⎰	head office
die Filiale (-n)	branch

2 Die Arbeitsbedingungen

Working conditions

die Probezeit	probationary period
die Ganztagsarbeit	full-time work
die Teilzeitarbeit	part-time work
er arbeitet Teilzeit	he works part time
die Gelegenheitsarbeit	casual work
als Aushilfssekretärin arbeiten	to temp
die gleitende Arbeitszeit	flexible working hours, flexitime
Überstunden machen	to do overtime
der Feierabend	end of work (for the day)
der Feiertag (-e)	day off, holiday
der Urlaub	holiday
sie arbeitet selbständig	she's self-employed
freiberuflich	self-employed
die Arbeitsplatzteilung	job-sharing
eine stumpfsinnige Arbeit	boring work/job
eine verantwortungsvolle Stelle	a responsible job
die Schichtarbeit	shift work
aufhören zu arbeiten	to retire
frühzeitig in den Ruhestand gehen	to take early retirement
die dynamische Rente	index-linked pension

im Pensionsalter	of retirement age

3 Finanzdinge

Financial matters

der Lohn (¨-e)	wage
das Gehalt (¨-er)	salary
das Prämiensystem	bonus scheme
die Beförderung	promotion
die Akkordarbeit	piecework
betriebliche Sozialleistungen	fringe benefits
die Gehaltserhöhung (-en)	pay rise
nach Abzug von Steuern	after tax
die Vergünstigung (-en)	perk
der Zahltag	pay day
der Mindestlohn	minimum wage
ihr Lohn liegt unter dem Existenzminimum	she's not earning a living wage
ein niedriges/mittleres Einkommen	a low/medium income

Der Familienhaushalt

Family budget

E

I Einkommen und Ausgaben

Income and expenditure

das Jahreseinkommen	annual income
die Ausgaben (*pl*)	outgoings
die Einkommensteuer (-n)	income tax
der Abzug (¨-e)	deduction (from wages)
die Steuervergünstigung (-en)	tax allowance
die Steuergruppe (-n)	tax bracket
die Miete (-n)	rent
eine Hypothek über DM200 000	DM200 000 mortgage
etw. auf Raten kaufen	to buy sth. on hire purchase
die Krankenversicherung (-en)	health insurance
die Lebensversicherung (-en)	life insurance
die Vollkaskoversicherung (-en)	comprehensive insurance
haftpflichtversichert sein*	to be insured third party
die Kreditkarte (-n)	credit card
die EC-Karte	direct debit card
der Anstieg der Lebenshaltungskosten	the rise in living costs
der Lebenshaltungskostenindex	cost-of-living index
die Kaufkraft	purchasing power
das ausgabefähige Einkommen	disposable income

der Lebensstandard	standard of living
die Begüterten	the well-off
die Einkommensstarken	
sie leben wie Gott in Frankreich	they live a life of luxury
sich nach der Decke strecken	to cut one's coat according to one's cloth
sich (Dat) den Gürtel enger schnallen	to tighten one's belt
über seine Verhältnisse leben	to live beyond one's means
seinen Verhältnissen entsprechend leben	to live within one's means
das kann ich mir nicht leisten	I can't afford that
die Armut	poverty
die Einkommensschwachen	those in a low income bracket
von der Hand in den Mund leben	to live from hand to mouth
in den roten Zahlen stecken	to be in the red
sie ist knapp bei Kasse	she's hard up
er hat Geldsorgen	he's got money problems
Geld allein macht nicht glücklich, aber es beruhigt	money alone doesn't make you happy, but it helps
das Geld aus dem Fenster werfen	to spend money like water

2 Die Banken — Banks

Geld verleihen	to lend money
das Darlehen (-)	loan
das Girokonto (-konten)	current account
die Kontoüberziehung (-en)	overdraft
das Konto ist überzogen	the account is overdrawn
der Kontoauszug (¨e)	bank statement
der Geldautomat (-e)	cash dispenser, cash machine
ich will das Geld auf mein Konto überweisen (ei-ie-ie) (insep)	I want to transfer the money to my account
einzahlen	to pay in
bar/mit Scheck bezahlen	to pay cash/by cheque
eine Schuld abzahlen/tilgen	to pay off a debt
einen Scheck auf jn. ausstellen	to make out a cheque to s.o.
eine Rechnung bezahlen	to settle a bill
Soll und Haben	debit and credit
sparen für, auf (+Acc)	to save for
mein Sparkonto bringt 7% Zinsen	my savings account pays 7% interest
die Kreditgrenze (-n) überschreiten	to go beyond one's credit limit

die Kreditkarte (-n)	credit card
der Scheck (-s)	cheque
sich Geld leihen (ei-ie-ie)	to borrow money
seine Bankgeschäfte telefonisch erledigen	to do one's banking by phone
die Geheimzahl eingeben	to tap in one's PIN
das Telefonat (-e)	phone call
vertraulich	confidential

Die Arbeitslosigkeit

Unemployment

F

I Das Problem

The problem

entlassen	to sack, dismiss
rausfliegen (*inf*)	to get the sack
100 Angestellte wurden entlassen	100 employees lost their jobs
die Kündigung	notice of dismissal
die natürliche Personalreduzierung	natural wastage
arbeitslos	unemployed
die Arbeitslosigkeit	unemployment
die Arbeitslosenzahlen steigen monatlich	the unemployment figures are rising month after month
eine Arbeitslosenrate von 6%	an unemployment rate of 6%
die Dunkelziffer	estimated number of unreported cases
betroffen sind vor allem ...	those most affected are ...
sich arbeitslos melden	to register as unemployed
die Arbeitslosenhilfe ⎤ das Arbeitslosengeld ⎦	unemployment benefit, dole
er ist auf Sozialhilfe angewiesen	he's dependent on state handouts
sie geraten in finanzielle Schwierigkeiten	they get into financial difficulties
die Selbstachtung	self-respect, self-esteem
die Frustration (-en)	frustration
überhöhte Lohnkosten	excessive wage costs
man hat die ganze Belegschaft Feierschichten machen lassen	they laid off the entire workforce
der ungelernte Arbeiter	unskilled worker
der angelernte Arbeiter	semi-skilled worker
der gelernte Arbeiter ⎤ der Facharbeiter ⎦	skilled worker
der Rationalisierungsschub	the drive to rationalise (working practices)

47

bestimmte Arbeitsplätze überflüssig machen	to make certain jobs superfluous
Arbeitsplätze gingen verloren	jobs were lost
Arbeitskräfte einsparen	to cut back on jobs
sie haben das Gefühl, nicht gebraucht zu werden	they have the feeling that they are not needed
es schlägt leicht in Apathie um	it easily turns into apathy
die Langzeitarbeitslosen	long-term unemployed

2 Gegenmaßnahmen *Counter-measures*

die Arbeitsbeschaffungsmaßnahmen (*pl*), ABM	job creation schemes
Maßnahmen zum Abbau der Arbeitslosigkeit	measures to reduce unemployment
die Kurzarbeit	reduction in working hours (to increase employment)
Gegenmaßnahmen ergreifen	to take counter-measures
die Umschulung	retraining
sich den veränderten Verhältnissen anpassen	to adapt to change
flexibel	adaptable, flexible
freie Arbeitsplätze	vacancies
die neuen Technologien (*pl*)	new technologies
neue Arbeitsplätze wurden geschaffen	new jobs were created
der Einsatz neuer Techniken	the introduction of new technologies
der Computer funktioniert reibungslos	the computer works efficiently
man muss die Produktion auf computergestützte Fertigung umstellen	production must be switched to computerised methods
mit dem technischen Wandel zurechtkommen	to cope with technological change
der Mangel an qualifizierten Arbeitskräften	shortage of qualified staff

G **Die Gewerkschaften** **Trade unions**

der Gewerkschaftler (-)	trade unionist
der Vertrauensmann ("-er)	shop steward
in den Streik treten*	to go on strike

einen Streik ausrufen	to call a strike
der Bummelstreik/Dienst nach Vorschrift	go-slow
wild streiken	to be on unofficial strike
eine Fabrik bestreiken	to black/go on strike at a factory
man hat vor der Fabrik Streikposten aufgestellt	they picketed the factory
die Kosten des Streiks werden auf ... beziffert	the cost of the strike is estimated at ...
die Gewerkschaft (-en)	trade union
ein vollorganisiertes Unternehmen	closed shop
der Lohnstopp	pay freeze
die Tarifverhandlungen	pay negotiations
die Tarife für Löhne kündigen	to put in a wage claim
der Tarifvertrag (-̈e)	pay agreement
höhere Löhne fordern	to demand higher wages
die Forderungen nach (+Dat)	demands for
die Schlichtungsverhandlungen (pl)	strike settlement negotiations
der Schlichtungsversuch scheiterte	the attempt at arbitration broke down
einen neutralen Schlichter einbeziehen	to call in an independent arbitrator
die Aussperrung	lock-out
die Arbeitszeitverkürzung	reduction in working hours
die Verlängerung des Urlaubs	lengthening the holiday

Frauen im Beruf / Women at work

das Kindergeld	family allowance
die Kinderkrippe (-n)	creche, nursery
die Gleichberechtigung	equal rights
gleicher Lohn für gleiche Arbeit	equal pay for equal work
wenn Frauen gleichwertige Arbeit wie Männer verrichten, dann sollten sie ...	if women do work equal in value to mens', they should ...
wie bewertet man die Arbeit?	how do you assess the value of the work?
Frauen sind Benachteiligungen ausgesetzt	women are subjected to discrimination
Schutzvorschriften für Schwangere	regulations to protect pregnant women
der Anteil von Frauen in ...	the proportion of women in ...

führende Positionen im
    Wirtschaftsleben

top executive positions

mehr Frauen mit Familie wollen
    zurück in den Beruf

more women with families want to
    go back to their careers

ein Prozess des Umdenkens

a rethinking process

sich verwirklichen

to fulfil oneself

die Frauenquote

proportion of jobs which must go
    to women

die sexuelle Belästigung

sexual harrassment

www.arbeitsamt.de
www.dgb.de

www.infoquelle.de
www.arbeit-online.de

Grundbegriffe

Basic terminology

A

die Konjunktur	economic situation
die Hochkonjunktur } der Aufschwung }	boom, upturn
Angebot und Nachfrage	supply and demand
der Gewinn (-e)	profit
der Verlust (-e)	loss
die freie Marktwirtschaft	free market economy
die soziale Marktwirtschaft	social market economy
die Konkurrenz	competition
die Rezession	recession
die Flaute (-n) (inf)	depression
die Zahlungsbilanz	balance of payments
der Verbraucher (-)	consumer
der Kunde (-n)	customer
der Großhandel	wholesale trade
der Einzelhandel	retail trade
die Wohlstandsgesellschaft	affluent society
die Verbrauchergesellschaft	consumer society
der Staat	the state
der Volkswirt	economist
der Existenzgründer (-)	entrepreneur
die Strategie (-n)	strategy
die Rechnung (-en)	invoice
die Bezahlung (-en)	payment
die Mahnung (-en)	reminder
Zulieferer und Abnehmer	suppliers and customers
der/die Sprecher/in	spokesman/woman
herstellen, erzeugen	to make, produce, manufacture
die Massenproduktion	mass production
Produktionsprozesse automatisieren	to automate production
computergesteuert	computer-controlled
am Fließband arbeiten	to work on the assembly line
fähig (person); leistungsfähig (machine)	efficient
einen Termin einhalten	to meet a deadline, keep an appointment
die Anforderung (-en)	requirement
der Lagerbestand	stock

die Lieferbedingungen (pl)	terms of delivery

B **Die Wirtschaftspolitik** — **Economic policy**

eine nachhaltige Verbesserung	a sustained recovery
die Aussichten (*pl*)	prospects
die Wirtschaftslage	economic situation
wir stehen vor erheblichen Problemen	we face considerable problems
der Haushaltsplan	budget
das Defizit	deficit
wirtschaftspolitisch sollte man ...	as far as economic policy is concerned, they ought to ...
die Wirtschaft ankurbeln	to boost the economy
das Wirtschaftsministerium	Department of Trade and Industry
die Steuer (-n)	tax
die Steuereinnahmen (*pl*)	revenue from taxation
das Finanzamt	Inland Revenue
das Steuerparadies	tax haven
die Steuern herabsetzen/ heraufsetzen	to lower/raise taxes
etw. mit Steuergeldern finanzieren	to finance sth. from taxpayers' money
brutto/netto	before/after tax, gross/net
die Mehrwertsteuer (MwSt)	value added tax (VAT)
die Einkommenssteuer	income tax
die Inflation bekämpfen	to fight inflation
die Bekämpfung der Inflation	the fight against inflation
die Voraussetzung für die Lösung aller wirtschaftlichen Probleme	the precondition for solving all economic problems
die Inflation ist zurückgegangen	inflation has fallen
die Zinssätze erhöhen	to raise interest rates
der Zinsanstieg	rise in interest rates
das Zinsniveau	level of interest rates
die Preise steigen*/sinken*/ schnellen* in die Höhe	prices are rising/falling/shooting up
die Preise erhöhen/herabsetzen	to raise/lower prices
eine ansteigende/rückläufige Tendenz	upward/downward trend
das Bruttosozialprodukt	gross national product (GNP)
die Produktion durch Subventionen fördern	to encourage production by means of subsidies

die Subvention (-en)	subsidy
subventionieren	to subsidise
verstaatlichen	to nationalise
privatisieren	to privatise
der öffentliche/private Sektor	public/private sector
in eine Krise geraten (ä-ie-a)*	to go into crisis
den Etat auf dem Vorjahresstand einfrieren	to freeze the budget at the same level as the previous year
etw. auf eine solide Grundlage stellen	to put sth. onto a firm footing
das Wirtschaftswunder	German post-war economic recovery

Der private Sektor — **The private sector**

I Die Firma — *The company*

die Firma (*pl* Firmen)	
das Geschäft (-e)	
das Unternehmen (-)	firm, company
die Gesellschaft (-en)	
der Betrieb (-e)	firm, company, factory
die Fabrik (-en)	factory
der multinationale Konzern (-e)	multinational company
der Dienstleistungsbetrieb (-e)	service industry
die Sparte (-n)	line of business
der Besitzer (-)	owner
der Leiter (-), der Chef (-s)	head, boss
der Direktor	director
der Aufsichtsrat	board
die Belegschaft	workforce
sich selbständig machen	to go into business
mit jm. ein Geschäft gründen	to go into business with s.o.
die Firma wurde 1950 gegründet	the firm was founded in 1950
an die Börse gehen	to float a company
der Leiter (-), der Manager (-)	manager
der Vertreter (-)	rep, salesman
der/die Sprecher/in	spokesman/woman
er leitet die Filiale in Dresden	he manages the branch in Dresden
der Jahresumsatz	annual turnover
die Konkurrenzfähigkeit	competitiveness
die Produktivität pro Kopf	output per head

die Waren (*pl*)	goods
das Angebot	goods on offer
der Auftrag (¨e) ⎱	order
die Bestellung (-en) ⎰	
die Lieferung (-en)	delivery
der Lieferant (-en)	supplier

2 Im Geschäft

In business

einen Termin mit jm. vereinbaren	to make an appointment with s.o.
für etw./jn Vorbereitungen treffen	to make arrangements for s.o./sth.
eine Besprechung/Konferenz/ Ausstellung organisieren	to organise a meeting/ conference/exhibition
vorgesehen; geplant	scheduled
der Treffpunkt	venue
die Tagesordnung	agenda
die Mitteilung (-en)	memo, report
jm. Bescheid sagen	to let s.o. know
die Dienstreise (-n)	business trip
der Flug (¨e)	flight
die Reservierung	booking
die Unterkunft	accommodation
stornieren; die Stornierung	to cancel; cancellation (reservation, order)
die Konferenz musste abgesagt werden	the meeting had to be cancelled
die Verspätung	delay
eine Frist einhalten (ä-ie-a)	to keep to a deadline
ein Auto mieten	to hire a car
das Protokoll; protokollieren	minutes; to take minutes
um Informationen über ... bitten	to request information on ...
sich erkundigen nach	to make an enquiry about
die Anfrage	enquiry
der Kostenvoranschlag	estimate of costs
zusammenfassen	to summarise
übersetzen (*insep*)	to translate
einer Anzeige folgen	to respond to an advertisement
sich beschweren	to make a complaint
mit einer Beschwerde fertigwerden	to deal with a complaint
bedauern	to regret
wir weisen darauf hin, dass ...	we wish to remind you that ...

die Verzögerung	delay
der Schaden/beschädigen	damage/to damage
die Versicherung kommt dafür auf	the insurance company pays for it

3 Angebot und Nachfrage

Supply and demand

das Geschäft wirft jetzt Gewin ab/rentiert sich	the company is now showing a profit
rentabel; die Rentabilität	profitable; profitability
den Umsatz steigern	to raise turnover
es herrscht starke Nachfrage nach ...	there is a great demand for ...
Nachfrage erzeugen	to create a market
auf dem Markt erscheinen	to come on to the market
den Markt überschwemmen	to flood the market
ein Markt mit starker Konkurrenz	a highly competitive market
das Produkt muss mit billigeren konkurrieren	this product has to compete against cheaper ones
sie gehen wie warme Semmeln weg (*inf.*)	they're selling like hot cakes
wie der Preis, so die Ware	you get what you pay for
das Geschäft blüht	business is booming
das Geschäft geht schlecht	business is slack
sie verkaufen es mit Verlust	they're selling it at a loss
die Produktion drosseln	to cut back on production
einen Betrieb stilllegen	to close down a factory
schließen (ie-o-o) (*itr*)	to close down
in finanzielle Schwierigkeiten geraten (ä-ie-a)*	to get into financial difficulties
Arbeitskräfte entlassen	to make workers redundant
Bankrott/Pleite machen	to go bankrupt
bankrott/pleite sein	to be bankrupt
zahlungsunfähig	insolvent
rückläufig	declining
um den Marktanteil kämpfen	to fight for a market share
der Marktführer (-)	market leader
DM50 000 Schulden haben	to be DM50 000 in debt
jm. einen Kredit von DM5 000 gewähren	to lend s.o. DM5 000
die Verkaufsziffern	sales figures
das Marketing	marketing
ein Produkt vermarkten	to market a product
die Marktforschung	market research

das Publicity-/Werbematerial	publicity materials
für ein Produkt werben (i-a-o)	to promote a product
die Marke (-n)	make, brand name
neue Kunden gewinnen	to win new customers
der Vorreiter sein	to be the first on the market
den Absatz steigern	to increase sales
jm 5% Rabatt auf etw. geben	to give s.o. 5% discount on sth.
zum halben Preis verkaufen	to sell at half price
der Großeinkauf	bulk purchase
der Schlussverkauf	sale, sell-off
das Sonderangebot	special offer
der Kundendienst	after-sales service
der Dienst am Kunden	customer service
sich beschweren bei jm.	to complain to
die Beschwerde (-n)	complaint
mit einer Beschwerde fertigwerden*	to deal with a complaint
die Verzögerung (-en)	delay
der Schaden/beschädigen	damage/to damage
die Versicherung	insurance
für etw. aufkommen	to pay for sth.

D · Die Börse / Stock exchange

der Kapitalanleger (-)	investor
der Börsenmakler (-)	stockbroker
der Aktionär (-e)	shareholder
die Aktie (-n)	share, share certificate
der Aktienindex	shares index
die Investition (-en)	investment
handeln mit	to deal in
sein Geld in ... anlegen	to invest in ...
(an der Börse) spekulieren	to speculate (on the stock exchange)
der Spekulant (-en)	speculator
die Spekulation mit Grundstücken	property speculation
an der Börse gehandelt	quoted on the stock exchange
der Börsensturz	collapse of share prices
der Markt erholt sich	the market is recovering
die Börse ist flau/lebhaft	trading is quiet/lively
die Fusion (-en)	merger
die Übernahme (-n)	takeover
das Übernahmeangebot (-e)	takeover bid

diese Firma ist eine gute Kapitalanlage	this company is a good investment
die Milliarde	a thousand million (US: billion)

Der internationale Handel — International trade

der Import/Export	import/export
importieren/exportieren	to import/export
die Handelsbilanz	balance of trade
die Zahlungsbilanz	balance of payments
das Außenhandelsdefizit	trade gap/deficit
verdeckte Einkünfte	invisible earnings
wie steht der Kurs momentan?	what's the rate of exchange at the moment?
das Handelsvolumen hat sich rasch vergrößert	trade has increased rapidly in volume
die Erholung ist auf die Belebung des Auslandsgeschäfts zurückzuführen	the recovery is due to the upturn in foreign trade
der Dollar ist stark gefallen	the value of the dollar has dropped sharply
eine harte Währung	a stable currency
die Währungsunion	monetary union
die Abwertung	devaluation
sein Anteil am gesamten Weltexport beträgt 5%	its share of world exports amounts to 5%
um seine Spitzenposition zu behaupten, ...	to maintain its leading position, ...
die BRD nimmt hinter den USA die zweite Stelle ein	Germany is in second place behind the USA
Großbritannien hat im Bereich Maschinenbau den Anschluss verpasst	Britain has missed the boat in the field of mechanical engineering
ihre Produkte sind qualitativ besser	their products are of better quality
sie sind auf britisches Know-how angewiesen	they rely on British know-how

www.bundesbank.de
www.zirn.de/urteile/bundesfinanzministerum.html
www.boerse.de

A Der Wahlkampf

die Redefreiheit	freedom of speech
ein vom Grundgesetz garantiertes Recht (-e)	a right guaranteed by the constitution
sich zur Wahl stellen	to stand for election
die Wählerschaft	electorate, constituents
das Wahlgeschenk (-e)	pre-election promise
einen Wahlkampf führen	to conduct an election campaign
Gott weiß was versprechen	to promise the earth
die Meinungsumfrage (-n)	opinion poll
30% der Befragten waren gegen die Regierung	30% of those polled were against the government
an Boden gewinnen	to gain ground
A holt B langsam ein	A is catching up with B
ihre Beliebtheit nimmt zu	she is gaining in popularity
Stimmen gewinnen/verlieren	to gain/lose support
jm. vertrauen	to trust s.o.
sich nach Moden richten	to follow the fashion
skeptisch	sceptical
seine Glaubwürdigkeit verlieren	to lose one's credibility
die Politikverdrossenheit	disenchantment with politics

B Die Wahlen

The election campaign

The elections

die Parlamentswahlen (*pl*)	general election
eine Wahl ankündigen	to call an election
ein Referendum abhalten (ä-ie-a)	to hold a referendum
das allgemeine Wahlrecht	right of every citizen to vote
stimmberechtigt	entitled to vote
das Wahlsystem	electoral system
das Mehrheitswahlrecht	'first past the post', majority voting system
das Verhältniswahlrecht	proportional representation
zu den Urnen gehen	to go to the polls
der Stimmzettel (-)	ballot paper
wählen	to vote
für einen Kandidaten stimmen	to vote for a candidate
eine hohe Wahlbeteiligung	a good turnout

ein überwältigender Sieg (-e)	a landslide victory
eine geringe/absolute Mehrheit	a small/absolute majority
ohne absolute Mehrheit	with no overall majority
das Wahlergebnis (-se)	election result
eine vernichtende Wahlniederlage	a crushing electoral defeat
er wurde zum Präsidenten gewählt	he was elected president
sie wurde in den Bundestag gewählt	she was elected to parliament
eine Koalition bilden	to form a coalition government

Die Staatsordnung

The system of government C

I Die Regierung

The government

die Staats- und Gesellschaftsordnung	system of government and social system
das Grundgesetz, die Verfassung	constitution
verfassungswidrig	unconstitutional
die Demokratie, demokratisch	democracy, democratic
an der Macht sein	to hold power
das Staatsoberhaupt (ᵉer)	head of state
der Parteichef (-s)	party leader
der Bundeskanzler (-)	Prime Minister
der Finanzminister (-)	Finance Minister/Chancellor of the Exchequer
der Innenminister (-)	Home Secretary/Minister of the Interior
der Außenminister (-)	Foreign Minister/Secretary
die Kabinettsumbildung	cabinet reshuffle
der Bundesrat	the Upper House (Lords)
der Bundestag (*Austria*: Nationalrat)	the Lower House (Commons)
der/die Abgeordnete (*adj. noun*)	member of parliament
ein Sitz (-e) im Parlament	seat in parliament
auf Bundesebene	at a national level

2 Die politischen Parteien

Political parties

die politische Partei (-en)	political party
die Parteienlandschaft	the political spectrum
über den Parteien stehen	to stand above politics
dem rechten Flügel der Partei angehören	to be on the right of the party
konservativ	conservative

liberal	liberal
der/die Gemäßigte (*adj. noun*)	moderate
der Sozialismus, sozialistisch	Socialism, socialist
die Sozialisten	labour
der Kommunismus, kommunistisch	Communism, communist
Bündnis 90, die Grünen	The Greens
der/die Links-(Rechts)radikale (-n)	left-(right-) wing extremist
totalitär	totalitarian
reaktionär	reactionary
revolutionär	revolutionary
kompromissbereit	prepared to compromise
das gegenwärtige System für gut halten	to be in favour of the present system

3 Das Parlament *Parliament*

die Sitzung (-en)	sitting
eine stürmische Debatte über ...	a stormy debate on ...
über einen Antrag (¨-e) abstimmen	to vote on a proposal
auf der Tagesordnung stehen	to be on the agenda
langfristige Maßnahmen (*pl*)	long-term measures
kuzfristige Maßnahmen (*pl*)	short-term measures
ein Gesetz (-e) entwerfen (i-a-o)	to draw up a bill
ein Gesetz (-e) einbringen	to introduce a bill
ein Gesetz (-e) verwerfen (i-a-o)	to throw out a bill
ein Gesetz (-e) verabschieden	to pass a bill
ein Gesetz (-e) aufheben (e-o-o)	to repeal an act
rechtskräftig werden	to become law
zurücktreten (i-a-e)*	to resign

Das politische Leben **Political life**

die straffe Führung	strong leadership
unter Leitung des Premierministers	under the leadership of the Prime Minister
vom Premierminister ernannt	appointed by the Prime Minister
radikale Maßnahmen ergreifen	to take radical measures
gegen die Inflation energisch vorgehen	to take a tough line on inflation
den Kopf in den Sand stecken	to bury one's head in the sand
die Sache schleifen lassen	to drag one's feet
Schwung verlieren (ie-o-o)	to lose momentum

er sieht den Wald vor lauter Bäumen nicht	he can't see the wood for the trees
sie hat ein klares Ziel vor Augen	she has a clear aim
eine durchgreifende Reform fordern	to demand a complete reform
die Reform zu einem Eckpfeiler seiner Politik machen	to make reform a cornerstone of one's policy
eine Diskussion auslösen	to provoke discussion
wegen der öffentlichen Kritik	due to public criticism
Fragen von weitreichender Bedeutung	questions of far-reaching importance
zu Auseinandersetzungen führen	to lead to disagreements
kontrovers	controversial
es birgt die Gefahr (-en), dass ...	it involves the danger that ...
die künftige Politik muss darauf abzielen, ...	future policy must aim to ...
eine aufrührerische Rede halten	to make an inflammatory speech
eine Tat (-en) verurteilen	to condemn an action
auf einen zunehmenden Widerstand stoßen (ö-ie-o)*	to meet with increasing resistance
sich weigern, nachzugeben	to refuse to back down
behaupten, dass zweimal zwei fünf ist	to argue that black is white
protestieren	to protest
eine Demonstration (-en) veranstalten	to hold a demonstration
die Unterschriftensammlung (-en)	petition
eine Kehrtwendung kritisieren	to criticise an about-turn
die Krise ist überwunden worden	the crisis has been resolved
in einer andauernden Krise stecken	to be in a continuing crisis

Die Kommunalverwaltung

Local government

die Gemeinde (-n)	local authority, local community
der Gemeinderat, Stadtrat (-̈e)	town council/councillor
der (Ober-)Bürgermeister (-)	(lord) mayor
die Gewerbesteuer (-n)	local business tax
die Gemeindeverwaltung	local authority
die Gemeindewahl	local elections

E

F

Die Europäische Union	The European Union
die gemeinsame Agrarpolitik	Common Agricultural Policy
eine Reform erzwingen	to force a reform
den Ausbau der Wirtschafts- beziehungen fördern	to promote the extension of economic links
die Wirtschaftsintegration	economic integration
die Währungsunion	single currency
der Mitgliedsstaat (-en)	member state
die Zusammenarbeit der Mitgliedsstaaten	the cooperation of member states
die föderative Struktur	federal structure
die Ausführung der Gemeinschaftsbeschlüsse durch die Mitgliedsstaaten	the implementation of Community decisions by member states
den Wohlstand der Bürger vermehren	to improve the prosperity of its citizens
die Europäische Kommission	European Commission
das Europäische Parlament	European Parliament
der Europäische Binnenmarkt	European internal market
die Europäische Zentralbank	European Central Bank
die Entscheidungsbefugnisse (pl)	decision-making powers
der Anteil am Welthandel	share of world trade
an der Spitze aller Handelsmächte stehen	to be the leading economic power
eine politisch handlungsfähige Union	a community capable of taking (joint) political action
die politische Unabhängigkeit einschränken	to limit political independence
am Entscheidungsprozess beteiligt sein	to be involved in the decision- making process
die Abhängigkeit der Landwirtschaft von Subventionen abbauen	to reduce the dependency of agriculture on subsidies
es führt zu Überschüssen (pl)	it leads to overproduction
steuerliche Schranken abbauen	to remove tax-barriers
Handelshindernisse abbauen	to remove barriers to trade
die Abschaffung der Grenzen	the removal of borders
der freie Verkehr von Personen, Waren, Dienstleistungen und Kapital	the free movement of people, goods, services and capital

Die deutsche Wiedervereinigung

German reunification

G

der Umbruch	upheaval, radical change
stürzen	to overthrow
das Ereignis (-se)	event
der Kalte Krieg	the Cold War
der Eiserne Vorhang	the Iron Curtain
der Demokratisierungsprozess	process of democratisation
Verhandlungen aufnehmen	to start negotiations
einen Vertrag billigen	to ratify a treaty
in Kraft treten	to come into force
zurücktreten (i-a-e)	to resign
schnelles Handeln war erforderlich	swift action was needed
die Übergangsfrist	transitional period
der Übergang zu einer Marktwirtschaft	the transition to a market economy
jm. etwas vorwerfen	to accuse s.o. of sth.
die NATO-Mitgliedschaft	NATO membership
Truppen (pl) abziehen	to withdraw troops
die Kosten der Einheit	the cost of unity
unterdrücken	to suppress, oppress
eine Demonstration gewaltsam zerschlagen	to break up a demonstration by violent means
die Überwachung	surveillance
inhaftieren	to arrest
die Geheimpolizei	secret police
der Spitzel (-)	informer
konkurrenzfähig	competitive
die ehemalige DDR	what used to be the GDR
der Wiederaufbau	reconstruction
den Regierungssitz von Bonn nach Berlin verlegen	to move the capital from Bonn to Berlin

www.bundestag.de	
www.austria.gv.at	*Austrian government website*
www.admin.ch	*Swiss government website*
www.firstlink.li	*Liechtenstein*

Die Außenpolitik

Foreign policy

internationale Beziehungen (*pl*)	international relations
diplomatische Beziehungen abbrechen	to break off diplomatic relations
die Botschaft/der Botschafter	embassy/ambassador
wirtschaftliche Sanktionen (*pl*) aufstellen gegen ...	to set up economic sanctions against ...
ein Ölembargo (-s) verhängen	to impose an oil embargo
die Großmächte (*pl*) die Supermächte (*pl*)	super-powers
die Atommächte	atomic powers
die Machtbalance	balance of power
die Macht ergreifen	to seize power
(über jn.) die Oberhand gewinnen	to gain the upper hand (over s.o.)
verhandeln über (+Acc)	to negotiate
das Gipfelgespräch	summit talks
über etwas Einigung erzielen	to reach agreement on sth.
ein Abkommen schließen	to sign a treaty
am Scheideweg stehen	to have reached a crossroads
das Scheitern der Verhandlungen	breakdown of talks
der Atomwaffensperrvertrag	nuclear non-proliferation treaty
sie kämpfen um ihre Freiheit	they're fighting for their freedom
in einem Streit vermitteln	to act as conciliator
die Friedenstruppen (*pl*)	peace-keeping force
Friedensverhandlungen führen	to hold peace talks
etw. vereinbaren	to agree on sth.
Maßnahmen zur Sicherung des Friedens	peace-keeping measures
die Entspannung	easing of tensions
die Beschwichtigung durch Zugeständnisse	appeasement
einen bedeutsamen Beitrag zu ... leisten	to make a significant contribution to ...
der Truppenabbau	troop reductions
Truppen abziehen	to withdraw troops
Truppen stationieren/einsetzen	to station/deploy troops

| die Abrüstung | disarmament |
| der Alliierte (*adj. noun*) }
der Allianzpartner (-) } | ally |

B

Krieg und Frieden

War and peace

I Der Krieg

War

den Krieg vermeiden	to avoid war
jm. den Krieg erklären	to declare war on s.o.
im Kreig stehen	to be at war
die militärische Intervention	military intervention
der Flüchtling (-e)	refugee
der Feind (-e)	enemy
für den Krieg rüsten	to arm for war
der Krieg zu Wasser, zu Lande und in der Luft	the war at sea, on land and in the air
die Schlacht (-en)	battle
der Kampf	battle, combat
verwüsten	to lay waste to
einen Krieg gewinnen (i-a-o)	to win a war
einen Sieg erringen (i-a-u)	to win a victory
besiegen	to defeat
sich (+Dat) unterwerfen	to submit to
erobern	to conquer
jm. ein Ultimatum stellen	to deliver an ulimatum to s.o.
einmarschieren in (+Acc)	to invade
die Invasion	invasion
angreifen (ei-i-i)	to attack
verteidigen	to defend
der Bürgerkrieg (-e)	civil war
gegeneinander kämpfen	to fight against one another
beschießen (ie-o-o)	to shell
umstellen (*insep*)	to surround
überrennen (*insep*) (*mixed verb*)	to overrun
die Niederlage (-n)	defeat
der Waffenstillstand	ceasefire
besetzen	to occupy (land)
die ethnische Säuberung	ethnic cleansing
Widerstand leisten	to offer resistance
verletzen	to wound
umbringen	to kill

viele kamen ums Leben	many lost their lives
überleben (insep)	to survive
der Gräuel (-)	atrocity
der Frieden (-)	peace

2 Die Streitkräfte — *The armed forces*

das Verteidigungsministerium	Ministry of Defence
Einsparungen (pl) im Verteidigungshaushalt	savings in the defence budget
die Bundeswehr	German Army
die Spionage	espionage
der Spion (-e)	spy
der Geheimdienst	secret service
der Spionagesatellit (-en)	spy satellite
die Armee, das Heer	army
die Truppen (pl)	troops
der Offizier (-e)	officer
marschieren	to march
das Gewehr (-e)	gun
der Panzer (-)	tank
die Marine	navy
das Kriegsschiff (-e)	warship
die Rakete (-n)	missile
der Marschflugkörper (-)	cruise missile
die Langstreckenwaffe (-n)	long-range weapon
die Luftwaffe	air force
das Kampfflugzeug (-e)	warplane
der Stützpunkt (-e)	base (air, naval, army)
konventionelle Waffen (pl)	conventional weapons
die Atomwaffen (pl)	atomic weapons
der Atomsprengkopf (¨e)	nuclear warhead
eine Atomstreitmacht sein	to possess a nuclear capability
biologische/chemische Waffen	biological/chemical weapons
das Atominferno	nuclear holocaust
die Massenvernichtung	mass destruction
die Abschrecken	deterrent
die allgemeine Wehrpflicht	national (military) service, conscription
seinen Militärdienst ableisten	to do one's military service
abschaffen	to abolish
der Berufssoldat (-en)	professional soldier

der Zivildienst	community service
der/die Zivildienstleistende	s.o. doing community work (rather
(*adj. noun*)	than military service)
der Kriegsdienstverweigerer (-)	conscientious objector
seinem Land dienen	to serve one's country
der Gemeinschaft dienen	to serve the community
der Pazifismus	pacifism
die Friedensbewegung	peace movement
der Waffenhandel	the arms trade

Der Terrorismus — Terrorism

das Attentat (-e)	terrorist attack
der Attentatsversuch (-e)	assassination attempt
kaltblütig	cold-blooded
wahllos angreifen (ei-i-i)	to strike indiscriminately
ein ziviles Ziel angreifen (ei-i-i)	to attack a civilian target
einen Anschlag verüben	to carry out an attack
sich zu einem Anschlag bekennen	to admit carrying out an attack
der Bombenanschlag (-̈e)	bomb attack
der Bombenalarm	bomb alert
ein Flugzeug entführen	to hijack a plane
der Entführer (-)	hijacker
die Geisel (-n)	hostage
die Geiselnahme	the taking of hostages
jn. als Geisel nehmen	to take s.o. hostage
der Fanatiker (-)	fanatic
foltern	to torture
der Gegenschlag (-̈e)	reprisal
eine versteckte Bombe	booby-trap bomb
großen Schaden anrichten	to cause great damage
das Opfer (-)	victim
einer Bombe zum Opfer fallen	to be the victim of a bomb
ermorden	to murder
politisch motiviert	politically motivated
rechts-/linksradikal	right-/leftwing extremist
unannehmbare Forderungen stellen	to make impossible demands
überall Abscheu auslösen/ hervorrufen	to provoke widespread disgust
Forderungen nachgeben	to give in to demands

einen festen Standpunkt vertreten	to take a firm stand
ausliefern	to extradite

Die Dritte Welt

The Third World

die Entwicklungsländer (*pl*)	developing countries
auf der Südhalbkugel	in the southern hemisphere
unterentwickelt	underdeveloped
die Armut bekämpfen	to fight poverty
die Entwicklungshilfe	development aid
das Elend lindern	to alleviate misery
das Wirtschaftswachstum	economic growth
die Schuldenkrise	debt crisis
der Geburtenzuwachs	increase in the birth rate
die Überbevölkerung	overpopulation
die Bevölkerungsexplosion	population explosion
niedrige Lebenserwartungen	low life-expectancy
Familienplanung betreiben	to practise family planning
die Geburtenkontrolle	birth control
der Geburtenüberschuss	excess of births over deaths
die Auslandsverschuldung	foreign debt
der krasse Unterschied zwischen arm und reich	the huge gulf between rich and poor
die ungleiche Verteilung	unequal distribution
der Analphabetismus	illiteracy
die Unterernährung	malnutrition
abgemagert	emaciated
unter der Armutsgrenze leben	to live below the poverty line
die Säuglingssterblichkeit	infant mortality
die Naturkatastrophe (-n)	natural disaster
die Überschwemmungen (*pl*)	floods
verhungern	to die of starvation
die Dürre (-n)	drought
die Hungersnot	famine
verwüsten	to lay waste to
das Erdbeben (-)	earthquake
der Erdrutsch (-e)	landslide
die Seuche (-n)	epidemic
eine 10 Meter hohe Flutwelle	a tidal wave 10m high
der Waldbrand (¨e)	forest fire
das Krisengebiet (-e)	crisis zone
die Hilfsorganisation (-en)	aid organisation

die Spende (-n)	contribution
zur Selbsthilfe anleiten	to help people to help themselves
Rohstoffpreise sichern	to guarantee prices for raw materials
fördern	to support, to aid

www.bmz.de
www.auswaertiges-amt.de
www.bundeswehr.de
www.epo.de

A — Die Verkehrspolitik / Transport policy

die öffentlichen Verkehrsmittel (pl)	public transport
das Verkehrsministerium	ministry of transport
das Straßennetz	road system
das Schienennetz	rail network
vorhanden	present, existing
das Netz ausbauen	to extend the network
das Straßenbauprogramm	road-building programme
die Neubaustrecke (-n)	new stretch (of road, track)
der Kanaltunnel	Channel Tunnel
sich an den Baukosten (pl) beteiligen	to share the building costs
die Kosten (pl) für etw. (+Acc) tragen	to bear the costs of sth.
die Sicherheit	safety
die Geschwindigkeit	speed
der Zeitgewinn	time-saving
der Fernverkehr	long-distance traffic/heavy goods
die Beförderung	movement (of goods)
die Strecke (-n)	route, stretch of road
die Grenze (-n)	border
die Verkehrspolitik richtet sich nach dem Auto	transport policy is geared to the car
den Individualverkehr auf öffentliche Verkehrsmittel verlagern	to get private transport users to use public transport
der Verkehrsverbund	integrated local transport system

B — Die Straßen / Roads

die Schnellstraße (-n)	express road
die Fernverkehrsstraße (-n)	trunk road
die Bundesstraße (-n)	'A' road
die Landstraße (-n)	'B' road
die Nebenstraße (-n)	side-road, minor road
das Autobahnkreuz (-e)	motorway junction, intersection
die (Autobahn)auffahrt (-en)	slip road (onto motorway)
die (Autobahn)ausfahrt (-en)	slip road (leaving motorway)

die Raststätte (-n)	service area
die Gebühr (-en)	toll
die geschlossene Ortschaft	built-up area
der Knotenpunkt (-e) ⎤	
die Kreuzung (-en) ⎦	crossroads, junction
die Einbahnstraße (-n)	one-way street
die Straße macht eine Kurve (-n)	there is a bend in the road
7km kurvenreiche Strecke	bends for 7km
nach rechts abbiegen* (ie-o-o)	to turn off to the right
die Straße macht eine Rechtskurve	the road bends to the right
die Ringstraße (-n)	ring-road
die Umleitung (-en)	diversion
einen Umweg machen	to make a detour
die Ortsumgehung (-en)	bypass
die Straßenbauarbeiten (*pl*)	roadworks
der Engpass (-pässe)	bottleneck

Der Straßenverkehr   **Road traffic**

der Verkehrsteilnehmer (-)	road user
der Nahverkehr	local traffic
das Fahrzeug (-e)	vehicle
das Kraftfahrzeug (Kfz)	motor vehicle
der Schwerlastverkehr	heavy goods traffic
der Güterverkehr	freight traffic
der Last(-kraft-)wagen (-), LKW	lorry truck
der Lastwagenzug (-̈e)	juggernaut (US: truck-trailer)
der Tankwagen (-)	tanker
der Lieferwagen (-)	van
mit dem Autoreisezug	by motorrail
die Zunahme (an +*Dat*)	increase (in)
den Verkehr lenken	to control/regulate traffic
die Verkehrsstauung (-en)	traffic jam
ein 20km langer Stau	a 20km long jam/tailback
eine hohe Verkehrsdichte	a high volume of traffic
verstopft	congested
die Spitzenzeiten (*pl*)	peak periods
die Hauptverkehrszeit	rush hour
der Berufsverkehr	rush hour traffic
die verkehrsreiche Straße	busy road
der ruhende Verkehr	stationary traffic
erhitzte/angespannte Gemüter (*nt pl*)	frayed tempers

C

Vorfahrt haben	to have the right of way

D

Der Individualverkehr	**Private transport**
1 Das Autofahren	*Driving*
der ADAC	=AA/RAC
den Führerschein bekommen	to get one's driving licence
der Führerschein auf Probe	driving licence for two-year probationary period (for all new drivers)
der PKW (Personenkraftwagen)	car (*official term*)
ein starkes Auto	powerful car
der Kombi (-s)	estate car
die Limousine (-n)	saloon (*US:* sedan)
unentbehrlich	essential, indispensable
verkehrssicher	safe, roadworthy
eine Panne haben	to break down
der geringe Benzinverbrauch	low petrol consumption
die Straßenverkehrsordnung	Highway Code
vorsichtig fahren	to drive carefully
Gas geben	to accelerate, put one's foot down
rückwärts fahren*	to reverse
bremsen	to brake
überholen (*insep*)	to overtake
Überholverbot	no overtaking
an jm. vorbeifahren*	to pass s.o.
mit 100 Stundenkilometern (km/h)	at 100 km.p.h
das Tempolimit	
die Geschwindigkeitsbegren- zung (-en)	speed limit
die Richtgeschwindigkeit	recommended speed limit (on motorways)
das Limit überschreiten	to exceed the speed limit
die Radarfalle	speed trap
der Sicherheitsgurt (-e)	seat belt
anschnallen	to fasten seat belts
die Anschnallpflicht	compulsory wearing of seat belts
einen Helm tragen	to wear a helmet
eine Panne haben	to break down
das Auto ist durch den TÜV gekommen	the car passed its MOT

2 Verkehrsverstöße

	Motoring offences
der Verkehrssünder	s.o. who has committed an offence
die Geldstrafe (-n)	fine
sie musste DM100 Strafe bezahlen	she was fined DM100
auf der Stelle	on the spot
sein Führerschein wurde entzogen	his licence was confiscated
er fährt zu dicht auf	he drives too close to the car in front
Abstand halten	to keep one's distance
verunglücken	to have an accident
einen Unfall verursachen	to cause an accident
auf etw. (+Acc) auffahren*	to drive into sth.
jn. überfahren (insep) (ä-u-a)	to knock s.o. down
der Zusammenstoß (¨-e)	crash
die Karambolage (-n)	multiple crash
frontal zusammenstoßen (ö-ie-o)*	to collide head-on
ins Schleudern geraten (ä-ie-a)*	to go into a skid
der Verkehrstote (-n)	road casualty
die Unfallrate senken	to reduce the number of accidents
ein Verkehrshindernis sein	to cause an obstruction

3 Das Parken

	Parking
auf dem Parkplatz	in the car park
das Parkhaus (¨-er)	multi-storey car park
die Tiefgarage (-n)	underground car park
der Strafzettel (-)	parking ticket (fine)
für alle Fahrzeuge gesperrt	closed to all vehicles
abschleppen	to tow away
die Radkralle (-n)	wheel clamp
den PKW-Verkehr aus den Innenstädten fernhalten	to ban cars from town centres

4 Die Mitfahrer

	Passengers
die Fahrgemeinschaft (-en)	car pool, car-sharing arrangement
das Trampen	hitch-hiking
jn. mitnehmen	to give s.o. a lift
jn. absetzen	to drop s.o. off
ich bringe dich zum Bahnhof	I'll take you to the station
sich auf den Weg machen	to set off, leave

Die öffentlichen Verkehrsmittel

Public transport

der Verkehrsverbund	integrated local transport network
die S-Bahn, Stadtbahn	high-speed urban railway
die Busspur (-en)	bus lane
die Busverbindungen (pl)	bus service
die Wochen-/Monatskarte (-n)	weekly/monthly travelcard
eine verbesserte Linienführung	better service
fahren, verkehren	to run (e.g. the bus runs)
im Stundentakt	at hourly intervals
der überfüllte Bus (-se)	crowded bus
der Busbahnhof (-e)	bus station
umsteigen*	to change
einen Anschluss (-e) verpassen	to miss a connection
halten (tr/itr) anhalten (tr/itr)	to stop

I Der Schienenverkehr

Rail traffic

das Schienennetz modernisieren	to modernise the rail network
das Defizit abbauen	to reduce the deficit
finanzielle Hilfen (pl)	financial help
verstärkte Investitionen (pl)	increased investment
eine Strecke stilllegen	to close down a line
wenig frequentiert	little used
belastet	heavily used
dem Schienen- gegenüber dem Straßenverkehr Priorität einräumen	to give rail traffic priority over road traffic
zuschlagpflichtig	supplementary fare payable
die Zeitkarte (-n)	season ticket
eine dichtere Zugfolge	more frequent train service

2 Der Flugverkehr

Air traffic

die Fluggesellschaft (-en)	airline
der Pendelverkehr	shuttle service
der Charterflug (-e)	charter flight
die Startbahn/Landebahn (-en)	runway
starten*	to take off
landen*	to land
abstürzen*	to crash

die Bruchlandung (-en)	crash-landing
die Flugleitung	air traffic control
der Luftraum	airspace
mit einer Höhe von ...	at an altitude of ...
der Fluggast (-e)	passenger
der Flugschreiber (-)	flight recorder, black box
der Zeitunterschied	time difference
der Jet-Lag	
die Schwierigkeiten durch }	jet lag
die Zeitumstellung	

Die Schifffahrt   Shipping   F

die Binnenwasserstraßen (pl)	inland waterways
die Binnenschifffahrt	inland shipping
der Lastkahn (-e)	barge
die Massengüter (pl)	bulk goods
die Werft (-en)	shipyard
die Hafenstadt (-e)	port
der Hafen (-)	harbour, docks, marina
eine Kreuzfahrt machen	to go on a cruise
auslaufen (äu-ie-au)*	to set sail
an Bord	on board
die Überfahrt (-en)	crossing, passage
die Seereise (-n)	voyage
der Liniendampfer (-)	liner
der Frachter (-)	freighter
Schiffbruch erleiden (ei-i-i)	to be (ship)wrecked
das Wrack (-s)	wreck
kentern*	to capsize
ertrinken (i-a-u)*	to be drowned
das Rettungsboot (-e)	lifeboat
die Gezeiten (pl)	tides
überqueren	to cross
auf Grund laufen	to run aground

Der Tourismus   Tourism   G

verreisen*	to go away (on trip, holiday)
die Anreise (-n)	the journey there
der Massentourismus	mass tourism
die Pauschalreise	package tour

der Pauschalurlauber (-)	s.o. on package holiday
der Reiseveranstalter (-)	tour organiser
die beliebtesten ausländischen Urlaubsziele	the favourite foreign holiday destinations
in der Hochsaison	in high season
die Nebensaison	off-peak
der Aufenthalt (-e)	stay
der Strandurlaub	beach holiday
der Badeort (-e)	seaside resort
der Kurort (-e)	health resort
der Tapetenwechsel	change of scene
ausspannen	to have a break
abschalten	to switch off
sich verwöhnen lassen	to allow oneself to be spoiled
das Bedürfnis nach Erholung	the need for relaxation
auf eigene Faust reisen	to travel independently
der Rucksackurlaub	backpacking holiday
Europa bereisen	to travel around Europe
andere Länder erleben	to get to know other countries
den Horizont erweitern	to broaden one's horizons
ein Stützpunkt für Fuss- und Autowanderungen	a base for walks and car trips
sich trimmen	to get fit
die Impfung (-en)	vaccination
sich impfen lassen	to have one's vaccinations
auf eigene Faust reisen	to travel under one's own steam
er ist verreist	he's away on holiday

www.bmv.de
www.tui-umwelt.com/deutsch/i/ib2.htm
www.lba.de
www.bahn.de

Der Computer | The computer

A

Many terms are identical in both English and German, with the gender given by the ending or the related German word (e.g. –er = masc; das Notebook (=das Buch))

Masc: Computer, Cursor, Cyberspace, Hacker, Laptop, Monitor, PC, Provider, Scanner, Server, Virus
Fem: CD-ROM, Diskette, E-Mail, Homepage, Hotline, Hardware, Software
Neut: Format, Icon, Keyboard, Modem, Notebook, Programm, Terminal, Update, World Wide Web

I Die Hardware	*hardware*
die Tastatur/das Keyboard	keyboard
der Speicher	memory
abspeichern/absaven	to save
die Festplatte (-n)	hard disk
die Diskette (-n)	floppy disk
der Drucker	printer
die Patrone (-n)	cartridge
die Maus (¨e)	mouse
der CD-Brenner	CD-writer
handlich	pocket-sized
2 Die Software	*software*
das Netzwerk	network
das Fenster	window
das Hauptmenu	main menu
das Verzeichnis (-se)	directory
anwenderfreundlich	user-friendly
das Anwenderprogramm	application program
die Textverarbeitung	word-processing
die Datenbank (-en)	database
die Shift-/Escape-Taste	shift/escape key
die Spacetaste/Leertaste	space key
anmelden/einloggen	to log on
abmelden/ausloggen	to log off
das Passwort, Kennwort (¨er)	password

abstürzen*	to crash
anklicken	to click on
aufrufen	to call up
aufrüsten/upgraden	to upgrade
ausdrucken	to print out
bearbeiten	to edit
der Befehl (-e)	command
booten/neustarten	to boot
die Datei (-en)	file
Datenkopien erstellen	to make a back-up
Das Datenschutzgesetz	data protection law
einblenden, einfügen	to insert
eingeben, eintippen	to enter (data), to key in
ein Programm installieren	to install a program
der Fehler (-)	bug
kleben	to paste
löschen	to delete
scannen/einscannen	to scan in
wiederfinden	to retrieve
die Papiermenge reduzieren	to reduce the volume of paper
die Schriftart (-en)	font
die Wissensexplosion	the information explosion
die künstliche Intelligenz	artificial intelligence
die Informationsgesellschaft	information technology-based society
Computer dringen in fast alle Lebensbereiche ein	computers affect almost every aspect of our lives
Computerviren vernichten den Datenbestand	computer viruses destroy stored data
Viren/einen Virus auffinden	to detect viruses/a virus
das Jahrtausendproblem	millennium bug

3 Das Internet	*The Internet*
im Internet surfen	to surf the net
der Internet-Nutzer (-)	internet user
die Internet-Adresse (-n) } die Webseite (-n) }	web-site
der Internet-Zugang	internet access
der Anschluss per Modem	link via a modem
die Datenübertragung	data transmission
die Suchmaschine (-n)	search engine

online sein*	to be online
die Online-Dienste	online services
die elektronischen Medien	the electronic media
auf Tastendruck	at the push of a button
die Kindersicherung	child protection
mit pornographischen Beiträgen konfrontiert werden	to be confronted with pornographic material
gewaltverherrlichend	violent (in content)
anstößige Inhalte aussortieren	to filter out offensive material
Klammeraffe	@
jm. mailen	to e-mail someone
downloaden/herunterladen	to download
uploaden/raufladen	to upload
der Info-Stress	information overload
die elektronischen Medien	electronic media

Die Bürotechnik | Office technology

fast alle Haushalte verfügen über ...	almost all homes have ...
das Ortsgespräch (-e)	local call
das Ferngespräch (-e)	long-distance call
neue Dienste anbieten	to offer new services
das Telefax	fax
das Faxgerät (-e)	fax machine
ein Dokument per Telefax schicken	to fax a document
die elektronische Post	electronic mail
die Büroarbeit rationalisieren	to make office work more efficient
die Telearbeit	networking
die Dezentralisierung	decentralisation
von Routinetätigkeiten entlasten	to free from routine chores
die Akte (-n)	file
der Aktenschrank (¨e)	filing cabinet
archivieren	to store
die Glasfaserkabel	optical fibre cable
über die Telefonleitung übermitteln	to transmit by telephone line
der Strichcode	bar code
das Handy (-s)	mobile phone
man ist immer erreichbar	people can always reach you
die Freisprechanlage (-n)	hands free kit (for mobile)
die Gesprächsgebühren (*pl*)	call charges
das schnurlose Telefon	cordless telephone

Die Industrie

Industry

die Fertigungstechnik	production technology
es unterliegt einem schnellen Wandel	it's undergoing rapid change
beschleunigen	to speed up
ersetzen	to replace
die Auswirkungen (*pl*) auf die Arbeitsplätze	effect on jobs
menschliche Arbeitskraft durch Technik ersetzen	to replace human labour by technology
Arbeitsplätze wegrationalisieren	to destroy jobs
die Fertigungsstraße (-n)	production line
am Fließband arbeiten	to work on the production line
Zeit- und Kostenaufwand verringern	to cut costs and time
der Technologiepark (-s)	science park
der Ausbau wachstumsstarker Technologien	the development of fast-growing technologies
die Forschung fördern	to support research

Die Forschung

Research

1 Allgemeine Begriffe

General concepts

Forschung und Entwicklung (FuE)	research and development (R&D)
forschen über (*+Acc*)	to research into
ein ressortübergreifendes Programm	a cross-disciplinary programme
neueste Forschungsergebnisse (*pl*)	latest research findings
Pionierarbeit für etw. leisten	to pioneer sth.
das Laboratorium (-rien) das Labor (-s)	laboratory
das Reagenzglas (-̈e)	test-tube
eine Methode perfektionieren	to perfect a technique
ein Problem lösen	to solve a problem
durch Ausprobieren	by trial and error
entwickeln	to develop
die Technik	technology
der Fortschritt (-e)	progress
an der Spitze stehen	to be in the lead
führend auf diesem Gebiet ist ...	the leader in this field is ...
verbessern	to improve
die Lebensqualität	quality of life
zurückliegen (ie-a-e)	to lag behind

Abhilfe schaffen	to take remedial action
die Innovation (-en)	innovation
ein Problem bewältigen	to overcome a problem
Wirklichkeit werden*	to become reality
eine neue Phase einleiten	to mark the start of a new phase
die Blaupause für ...	the blueprint for ...
mit der herkömmlichen Technik	with present-day technology
bis zum Jahre 2020 wird man ...	by the year 2020 they'll ...
muss man alles machen, was machbar ist?	do we have to do everything just because it's possible?
die meisten Menschen wollen nicht zum Sklaven der modernen Technik werden	most people don't want to become slaves of modern technology

2 Die Weltraumforschung

Space research

der Weltraum, das All	space
der Raumflug (-̈e)	space flight
der Raumtransporter (-)	space shuttle
die Umlaufbahn (-en)	orbit
die Raumsonde (-n)	space probe
die Weltraumwaffe (-n)	space weapons
neue Erkenntnisse gewinnen (i-a-o)	to gain new knowledge
ein uralter Traum	an ancient dream
die Raumstation (-en)	space station

3 Die medizinische Forschung

Medical research

die Pharmaindustrie	pharmaceutical industry
einen Versuch machen	to carry out an experiment
die minimal invasive Chirurgie/ Schlüssellochchirurgie	keyhole surgery
neue Operationstechniken erproben	to try out new surgical techniques
die Genauigkeit erhöhen	to improve the accuracy
Neben- und Nachwirkungen	side- and after-effects
der Behandlungserfolg (-e)	successful treatment
Versuche an Tieren einstellen	to halt experiments on animals
genehmigen	to permit
rechtfertigen	to justify
die Kosmetika (*pl*)	cosmetics
jn. quälen	to inflict suffering on s.o.
die Risiken (*pl*) für den Patienten vermindern	to lower the risks to the patient

81

als Versuchskaninchen verwenden	to use as a guinea-pig
sich einer Organverpflanzung unterziehen (ie-o-o; *insep*)	to undergo an organ transplant
ein geschädigtes Organ ersetzen	to replace a damaged organ
der Spender (-)	donor
der Empfänger (-)	recipient
das Organ abstoßen (ö-ie-o)	to reject the organ
der Herzschrittmacher	pace-maker
zur Routine werden*	to become routine

4 Die Gen-Technologie   *Genetic engineering*

Mikroorganismen (*Dat pl*) neue Eigenschaften verleihen (ei-ie-ie)	to give microorganisms new characteristics
der DNS-Code	DNA code
der Embryo (-nen)	embryo
Experimente mit menschlichen Embryonen	experiments on human embryos
das Retortenbaby (-s)	test-tube baby
die Heilung von Erbkrankheiten	the treatment of hereditary disease
das menschliche Erbgut manipulieren	to manipulate human genetic make-up
zu ... Zwecken	for ... purposes
die Unantastbarkeit/Heiligkeit des ungeborenen Lebens	the sanctity of the unborn child
ethische Bedenken (*pl*)	ethical considerations
eine Krankheit ausmerzen	to eradicate a disease
die Nachweismethode	detection technique
eine Methode einsetzen	to use a technique
die Überlebensrate steigern	to raise the survival rate
die Zulassung neuer Medikamente	the licensing of new drugs
gentechnisch veränderte Nahrungsmittel	genetically modified food
Anbau, Ertrag und Haltbarkeit verbessern	to improve cultivation, yield and shelf-life
der Klon (-e), klonen	clone, to clone

www.stifterverband.de	www.bmbf.de
www.dlr.de	www.intel.de

Die Umwelt

Die Probleme

The problems

die Umwelt	environment
der Umweltschutz	environmental conservation
schützen (vor +Dat)	to protect (from)
umweltfreundliche Produkte (pl)	environmentally friendly products
umweltfeindlich	damaging to the environment
konsumieren, verbrauchen	to consume, use
künstlich	artificial
im Laufe unseres Lebens	in the course of our lives
die Gefährdung (+Gen)	danger (to)
die Verschmutzung	pollution
verschmutzen, belasten ⎫ verpesten, verseuchen ⎭	to pollute
voll/frei von Schadstoffen	full/free of harmful substances
vernichten, zerstören	to destroy
verschwenden	to waste
schaden (+Dat)	to damage
vergiften	to poison
durch natürliche oder vom Menschen ausgelöste Faktoren verursacht	from natural or man-made causes
der Umweltsünder (-)	polluter

Die Folgen

The consequences

in den Naturhaushalt eingreifen (ei-i-i)	to upset the balance of nature
es hat beängstigende Ausmaße erreicht	it has reached a worrying level
man sagt voraus, dass ...	it is forecast that ...
die Folgen (pl) voraussagen	to predict the consequences
die Folgen sind kaum absehbar	it's hard to say what the consequences will be
bis zum Beginn des nächsten Jahrhunderts	by the beginning of the next century
um kommender Generationen willen	for the sake of future generations
das wird uns teuer zu stehen kommen	that will cost us dear

schädliche Auswirkungen (pl)	harmful effects
es wird Millionen in das Elend stürzen	it will plunge millions into poverty
vor etw. (+Dat) warnen	to warn of sth.
die Katastrophe (-n)	disaster
was bleibt übrig?	what's left?
zurückgreifen auf (+Acc)	to fall back on
rücksichtslos	thoughtless
gesundheitsgefährdend	damaging to health
katastrophale Auswirkungen (pl)	catastrophic effects
die Immission	effect on people, plans, buildings of noise, pollution, etc.
gefährden	to endanger
vom Aussterben bedrohte Tierarten	species threatened with extinction
die Bedrohung der Menschen	threat to humanity

C **Die Gegenmaßnahmen**

Counter-measures

die Schadstoffbelastung mindern	to reduce damage by pollutants
die Schäden (pl) eindämmen	to contain the damage
der Umweltverstoß (-̈e)	action damaging to the environment
die Umwelterziehung	environmental education
auf die Umweltverschmutzung aufmerksam machen	to raise awareness of environmental pollution
das Umweltbewusstsein	environmental awareness
eine Wende in der öffentlichen Einstellung zum Umweltschutz	a change in the public's attitude to environmental conservation
wir müssen schon entstandene Schäden (pl) beseitigen	we must repair damage which has already been done
wenn zu ihrer Rettung nichts unternommen wird	if nothing is done to save them
Gegenmaßnahmen (pl) einleiten	to introduce counter-measures
grenzüberschreitende Regelungen (pl)	cross-border agreements
das Gesetz verschärfen	to tighten up the law
den Umweltschutz in die Praxis umsetzen	to put environmental conservation into practice
sich zu etw. verpflichten	to commit oneself to sth.
ökonomische und ökologische Interessen abwägen	to balance economic and ecological interests

... gilt als unverzichtbar	... is thought to be indispensable
vorsorglich	as a precaution
mit etw. sparsam umgehen	to use sth. economically
retten	to save
schützen	to protect
wir sind von ... (+Dat) abhängig	we depend on ...
es gibt kein Zurück	there's no going back
um das Überleben der Menschheit zu sichern	in order to ensure the survival of humanity
sparsam im Verbrauch	economical
... stellt ein Problem für die Industrie dar	... represents a problem for industry
die langfristigen Auswirkungen bewerten	to assess the long-term effects
... hätte zur Folge, dass ... ⎫ ... hätte den Effekt, dass ... ⎬	... would have the effect that ...
die Umweltkarte	cheap tickets to encourage use of public transport
die Umweltsteuer, Ökosteuer (-n)	environmental tax

Die Luft

Air

die Emission (-en)	emission (of gas, etc.)
der Wasserstoff	hydrogen
der Sauerstoff	oxygen
der Stickstoff	nitrogen
der Kohlenstoff	carbon
das Kohlendioxid	carbon dioxide, CO_2
das Schwefeldioxid	sulphur dioxide, SO_2
giftige Abgase (pl) abgeben	to give off poisonous waste gases
in die Atmosphäre blasen	to pump into the atmosphere
freisetzen	to release
quellen (i-o-o)* aus	to pour from
das Gift (-e)	poison
das Auspuffrohr (-e)	exhaust pipe (of vehicle)
der saure Regen	acid rain
das Waldsterben	widespread destruction of forests by acid rain
ehemals dichtbewaldete Flächen (pl)	what were once thickly forested areas
die Korrosionsschäden (pl) an Gebäuden	corrosion damage to buildings

die Bodenerosion	soil erosion
es entsteht durch ...	it results from ...
die Spray-Dose (-n)	aerosol
sprühen	to spray
die FCKW (*pl*) (Fluorchlorkohlenwasserstoffe)	CFCs (chlorofluorocarbons)
das Treibgas	propellant (in aerosol)
das Kühlmittel (-)	coolant
die Ozonschicht	ozone layer
das Ozonloch	hole in the ozone layer
ultraviolette (UV) Strahlen (*pl*)	ultraviolet (UV) rays
ein vermehrtes Auftreten von Hautkrebs	an increased incidence of skin cancer
die Erwärmung der Erdatmosphäre	global warming
der Treibhauseffekt	greenhouse effect
die Klimaveränderungen (*pl*)	changes to the climate
der Anstieg des Meeresspiegels	rise in sea-level
das Abschmelzen der Polkappen	melting of ice-caps
die Überflutung der Küstenstreifen	flooding of coastal regions
die Dürre	drought
verbleit/bleifrei tanken	to use leaded/lead-free petrol
der Katalysator	catalytic convertor
der Ruß	soot
der Krebsauslöser	cancer-causing agent, carcinogen
krebserregend	carcinogenic (*adj*)
Autos müssen reduzierten Abgasnormen genügen	cars have to meet stricter exhaust controls
die Steuervorteile (*pl*)	tax incentives
der geringe Benzinverbrauch	low fuel consumption
die Verkehrsberuhigung	building a road so that high speeds are impossible/"traffic-calming"
Autofahrer am Rasen hindern	to make drivers slow down
die Geschwindigkeitsbegrenzung (-en)	speed limit

Das Wasser

Water

der Stausee (-n)	reservoir
in das Grundwasser sickern	to seep into the ground water
die Wasservorräte (*pl*)	water reserves
die Wasserversorgung	water supply

Chemikalien ins Gewässer ablassen	to release chemicals into rivers, lakes
einen Ölteppich beseitigen	to clean up an oil slick
das Abwasser	sewage
die Kläranlage (-n)	sewage treatment plant
industrielle Abwässer (pl)	industrial effluent
die Aufnahmekapazität des Meeres für Schadstoffe	ability of the sea to absorb pollutants
die Anrainerstaaten (pl) der Nordsee	countries bordering on the North sea

Der Boden   The soil

die Landwirtschaft	agriculture
hohe Nitratgehalte (pl)	high concentrations of nitrates
in Gebieten mit intensiver Landwirtschaft	in areas with intensive agriculture
die steigende Agrargüter-Erzeugung	rising agricultural production
künstliche Düngemittel (pl) verwenden	to use artificial fertilisers
den Boden belasten	to pollute the soil
die Rückstände (pl)	residues
die Entwässerung	drainage
die Ansammlung von Pestiziden (pl) im Boden	the build-up of pesticides in the soil
Schadstoffe gelangen* über die Nahrungskette in den Körper	pollutants reach the body by way of the food chain
die Bio-Lebensmittel (pl)	organic food
die ökologische Landwirtschaft	organic agriculture
der Rohstoffabbau	mining of raw materials
den Regenwald vernichten	to destroy the rain forest
mit Urwald bedeckt	covered with virgin forest
das Land/den Wald roden	to clear land/forest
die Entwaldung	deforestation
das Naturschutzgebiet (-e)	nature reserve
ein empfindliches Öko-System	a delicate ecosystem
gefährdete Tier- und Pflanzenarten	threatened animal and plant species
aussterben (i-a-o)*	to become extinct
ausrotten	to exterminate

Der Müll	**Rubbish**
der Sperrmüll	bulky items of refuse
die Sondermüllsammelstelle (-n)	collection point for old paint, oil, etc.
die Müllabfuhr	refuse collection
die Abfallentsorgung	waste disposal
die Mülldeponie (-n)	rubbish dump
die Müllverbrennungsanlage	refuse incinerator plant
den Müll getrennt sammeln	to collect types of rubbish separately
die Abfalltrennung	separation of rubbish into plastics, paper, etc.
es kommt alles in den Mülleimer	it all goes into the dustbin
wegschmeißen ⎫	
wegwerfen ⎭	to throw away
die wilde Müllkippe (-n)	illegal rubbish dump
die Verklappung	dumping of industrial waste at sea
die Plastiktüte (-n)	plastic bag
Abfälle auf die Straße werfen	to drop litter in the street
der Kunststoffcontainer (-)	plastic container
die Einwegflasche (-n)	non-returnable bottle
die Mehrwegflasche (-n)	returnable bottle
die Pfandflasche (-n)	returnable bottle
die Alu-Dose (-n)	aluminium can
der Schrott	scrap metal
der Autoschrott	scrap cars
leere Flaschen zum Altglascontainer bringen	to take empty bottles to the glass recycling skip
das Recycling	recycling
wiederverwerten	to recycle
wiederverwertbar	recyclable
der Mangel an Rohstoffen (pl)	the shortage of raw materials
Rohstoffe (pl) wiedergewinnen	to reclaim raw materials
aus Altpapier	made from recycled paper
fertigen	to manufacture
zu neuen Produkten verarbeiten	to turn into new products
die Kartonage (-n)	cardboard packaging
die Verpackungen (pl)	packaging
biologisch abbaubar	bio-degradable
die Abfallvermeidung	ways of reducing amount of waste

H

Die Energie	Energy
I Fossile Brennstoffe	*Fossil fuels*
der Energiebedarf	energy requirements
der Energieverbrauch	energy consumption
die Kohle	coal
das Gas	gas
das Öl	oil
die Erdölförderung	oil production
erschöpft werden	to run out
das Rohöl	crude oil
der Preis fiel auf $x je Barrel	the price fell to $x a barrel
das Benzin	petrol, gas (*USA*)
der Dieselkraftstoff	diesel fuel
die Erdölförderländer (*pl*)	oil-producing countries

2 Die Atomenergie	*Atomic energy*
die Kernenergie	atomic energy
das Kernkraftwerk (KKW)	nuclear power station
der Brennstoff	fuel
die Brennstäbe (*pl*)	fuel rods
der GAU (Größter anzunehmender Unfall)	MCA (maximum credible accident)
das Kernschmelzen	meltdown
die Strahlung	radiation
sollten wir das Risiko eingehen?	should we take the risk?
zum Antrieb von Turbinen einsetzen	to use to drive turbines
die Wideraufbereitungsanlage (WAA)	nuclear reprocessing plant
der Kernreaktor, der Atomreaktor	nuclear reactor
die Endlagerung radioaktiver Abfälle	the storage of radioactive waste
ein Atomkraftwerk stilllegen	to close down a nuclear power station
ein Atomkraftwerk in Betrieb nehmen	to commission a nuclear power station

3 Erneuerbare Energiequellen	*Renewable energy sources*
alternative Energiequellen entwickeln	to develop alternative energy sources
energiesparend	energy-saving

der globale Energieverbrauch	total energy consumption
die Wasserkraft	hydroelectric power
die Sonnenenergie	solar energy
die Solarzellen	solar cells
die Windenergie	wind power
die geothermische Energie	geothermal energy
die Wellenenergie	wave power
die Gezeitenenergie	tidal power
das ist hier nicht zu verwirklichen	this could not be put into effect here
sie werden schon kommerziell betrieben	they are already in commercial use
sie können nicht kontinuierlich Energie liefern	they cannot supply energy constantly
ihr Einsatz wird eingeschränkt durch ...	their use is limited by ...
der Ausbau dieser Anlagen wird vorgesehen	further building of these plants is planned
den Verbrauch auf das Nötigste einschränken	to limit consumption to the minimum

4 Konservierung zu Hause   *Conservation at home*

die Isolierung	insulation
isolieren	to insulate
große/geringe Energiegewinne (*pl*)	large/small energy savings
die Doppelfenster (*pl*)	double glazing
die dreifache Verglasung	triple glazing
die Regelanlage einstellen	to adjust the time/temperature unit
lüften	to ventilate
schonen	to conserve
dadurch könnte man bis zu 20% Energie sparen	by this method energy savings of up to 20% could be made
auf etw. verzichten	to do without sth.
ein besserer Ausnutzungsgrad	more efficient use

www.geowissenschaften.de
www.esso.de
www.tui-umwelt.com/deutsch/start.htm
www.verreisen.de

These place names sometimes cause difficulty

die Ostsee	Baltic Sea
der Pazifik	Pacific Ocean
der Kanal/Ärmelkanal	the Channel
das Mittelmeer	Mediterranean Sea
der Bodensee	Lake Constance
die Donau	River Danube
der Rhein	River Rhine
die Themse	River Thames
Aachen	Aachen, Aix-la-Chapelle
Brügge	Bruges
Brüssel	Brussels
Dünkirchen	Dunkirk
Genf	Geneva
Genua	Genoa
den Haag	The Hague
Köln	Cologne
Lüttich	Liege
Mailand	Milan
Moskau	Moscow
Mülhausen	Mulhouse
München	Munich
Neapel	Naples
Nizza	Nice
Nürnberg	Nuremberg
Straßburg	Strasbourg
Venedig	Venice
Warschau	Warsaw
Wien	Vienna
Lettland	Latvia
Siebenbürgen (in Rumänien)	Transylvania
der Nahe Osten	the Middle East
der Ferne Osten	the Far East

 www.kommon.de/staedte.htm

Die Stadt

die Stadt Stuttgart	city of Stuttgart
die Stuttgarter (-er *invar*) Kirchen	Stuttgart's churches
der Einwohner (-)	inhabitant
der Stadtbewohner (-)	town-dweller
die städtische Bevölkerung	the urban population
der Bürger (-)	citizen
die Großstadt (¨e)	city, large town
die Verwaltung (-en) ⎫ die Behörde (-n) ⎭	administration, authorities
das Ballungsgebiet (-e)	conurbation
die Schlafstadt (¨e)	dormitory town
einen Stadtbummel machen	to go for a stroll around town
das kulturelle Leben	cultural life
zentral gelegen	situated in the town centre
die städtische Lebensweise	city way of life
die Infrastruktur	infrastructure
von ... umgeben	surrounded by ...

The town

Die Städteplanung

die Stadtmitte ⎫ das Stadtzentrum (-zentren) ⎭	town centre
die Altstadt (¨e)	old part of town
das Stadtbild	features of the town
der Stadtrand	outskirts
die Vorstadt (¨e)	suburbs
bebaut	built-up
das Stadtviertel (-)	district
das Wohngebiet (-e)	housing area
die Wohnsiedlung (-en)	housing estate
das Industriegebiet (-e)	industrial estate
das Gebäude (-)	building
das Hochhaus (¨er)	skyscraper
die Zentrale (-n)	head office
das Lagerhaus (¨er)	warehouse
die Fabrik (-en)	factory
der Wohnblock (¨e)	block of flats

Town planning

das Wohnsilo (-s)	rabbit hutches (pej)
das möbilierte Zimmer (-)	bedsit
das Einkaufszentrum (-zentren)	shopping centre
die Fussgängerzone (-n)	pedestrian zone
die Passage (-n)	shopping arcade
der Bürgersteig	pavement

Wohnungen

Housing

C

der Städtebau	urban development
der Wohnungsbedarf	housing needs
der Wohnungsmangel die Wohnungsnot	housing shortage
heimatlos	homeless
die Wohnverhältnisse (pl)	living conditions
das Wohnungsbauprogramm	housing programme
instandsetzen	to repair
instandhalten	to maintain
modernisieren	to modernise
vernachlässigen	to neglect
abreißen (ei-i-i)	to pull down
einstürzen*	to fall down
baufällig	dilapidated, unsafe
der Immobilienmakler (-)	estate agent
das Einzelhaus (¨er)	detached house
das Fertighaus (¨er)	prefabricated/kit house
vorfertigen	to prefabricate
der Beton	concrete
wohnlich	homely, cosy
die Wohngemeinschaft (-en)	people sharing house
der Hausbesetzer (-)	squatter
besetzen	to occupy
besitzen (i-a-e)	to own
der Mieter (-)	tenant
der Vermieter (-)	landlord
die Miete (-n)	rent
die Eigentumswohnung (-en)	owner-occupied flat
etw. steuerlich fördern	to give tax incentives for sth.
die Sozialwohnung (-en)	council flat
leerstehen	to stand empty
die Baustelle (-n)	building site
der Bedarf an Bauland	the need for building land

das Grundstück (-e)	building plot
die Hypothekenzinsen (*pl*)	mortgage rates
sanieren	to clean up, renovate
die Straßenbeleuchtung	street lighting
verschönern	to beautify

D **Probleme** — **Problems**

der Härtefall (¨-e)	case of hardship
die Armut	poverty
der Trend zu Einpersonenhaushalten	the trend towards single-person households
das Elendsviertel (-)	slums
die Barackensiedlung (-stadt)	shanty town
das Ödland	wasteland
der Straßenraub	mugging (category of crime)
der Überfall (¨-e)	mugging (incident)
betteln	to beg
schnorren (*inf*)	to scrounge
der Bettler (-)	beggar
der Stadtstreicher (-)	vagrant
die Stadtstreicherei	vagrancy
obdachlos	homeless
ohne festen Wohnsitz	of no fixed abode
im Freien übernachten	to sleep rough
von Zuhause weglaufen	to run away from home
die Betonwüste	concrete jungle
die Einsamkeit	loneliness
benachteiligt	deprived
von der Hand in den Mund leben	to live from hand to mouth
die Anonymität	anonymity
die Gesellschaft	company (of other people)
der Pendler (-)	commuter
der Berufsverkehr	commuter/rush hour traffic
die Stadtflucht	exodus from the cities
die Bodenpreise schnellen* in die Höhe	land prices are going through the roof
die Hektik, das Gedränge	hustle and bustle

E **Die Landwirtschaft** — **Agriculture**

der Landbewohner (-)	country dweller

der Bauer (-)/Bäuerin (-nen) }
der Landwirt (-e) }   farmer

der Kleinbauer	smallholder
der Großbetrieb (-e)	large farm
erben	to inherit
das Bauerndorf (¨er)	farming community
die Landwirtschaft	agriculture
pflügen	to plough
ernten	to harvest
die Ernte (-n)	harvest
der Mähdrescher (-)	combine harvester
säen	to sow
anbauen	to grow sth.
das Getreide	cereal crops
der Weizen	wheat
der Getreideanbau	arable farming
die Milchviehhaltung	dairy farming
der Rinderwahnsinn	mad cow disease, BSE
eine Übertragung des Rinderwahnsinns auf den Menschen kann nicht ausgeschlossen werden	the transmission of mad cow disease to humans cannot be ruled out
die künstlichen Düngemittel	artificial fertilisers
das Feld (-er)	field
die Wiese (-n)	meadow
der Winzer (-) } der Weinbauer (-) }	wine-grower
der Weinberg (-e)	vineyard
die Weinlese (-n)	grape harvest
die Forstwirtschaft	forestry
Bäume einschlagen/fällen	to fell trees
den Wald roden	to clear forest land
wiederaufforsten	to reforest
das Wild	game
staatliche Hilfen	state subsidies
die Massentierhaltung	intensive livestock farming

Die Zukunft   ## The future

die Flurbereinigung	reparcelling of agricultural land into fields of economic size
rentabel	economic

leistungsfähig	efficient
die zunehmende Mechanisierung	increasing mechanisation
der Pächter (-)	tenant farmer
verpachten	to lease out
die Genossenschaft (-en)	cooperative
die gemeinsame Agrarpolitik	Common Agricultural Policy (CAP)
die Quoten (*pl*) für die Milcherzeugung	milk production quotas
die Nahrungsmittelproduktion	food production
die Überschussproduktion drosseln	to cut back surplus production
aus der landwirtschaftlichen Nutzung herausnehmen	to set aside (from agricultural use)
das Land ökologisch bewirtschaften	to farm organically
die Flächenstilllegung	'setting aside' agricultural land

Auf dem Land leben	**Living in the country**
wo sich Fuchs und Hase „Gute Nacht" sagen	in the sticks
das Erholungsgebiet	holiday/recreation area
unberührte Natur erleben	to enjoy unspoiled countryside
der Berggipfel (-)	mountain top
bergig	mountainous
die Küste (-n)	coast
die Bucht (-en)	bay
geruhsam	peaceful, leisurely
man ist aufs Auto angewiesen	people are dependent on the car
die Landflucht	rural depopulation
die Strukturschwäche in ländlichen Gebieten	rural deprivation

www. www.d-berlin.de
www.bmlf.gv.at
www.entry.de

Die Rechtsordnung

Note that there are many differences between the German legal system and those of Britain or the USA; take great care when looking for equivalents in, for instance, courts or procedures.

Die Rechtsordnung	Legal system
der Rechtsstaat	the rule of law
das Recht	justice, legal system
das Recht (-e)	right
das Völkerrecht	international law
die Menschenrechte (pl)	human rights
einen Rechtsanspruch auf etw. haben	to be within one's rights to do sth.
die Gerechtigkeit	justice
(un-)gerecht	(un-)just
das Recht beanspruchen, etw. zu machen	to claim the right to do sth.
der Bürger wird dadurch in seinen Rechten verletzt	this violates basic civil rights
das Gesetz (-e)	law, statute
das Arbeitsrecht	labour law
die Verordnung (-en)	by-law
etw. für rechtmäßig erklären	to make sth. legal
in Kraft treten (i-a-e)*	to come into force
gesetzlich	by law
etw. kriminalisieren	to make sth. a criminal offence
legalisieren	to legalise
schützen vor (+Dat)	to protect from
das Gericht (-e)	court
das Bundesverfassungsgericht	constitutional court
die Todesstrafe abschaffen	to abolish the death penalty
der Prozess (-e)	trial
der Jurist (-en)	lawyer
der Richter (-)	judge
der Staatsanwalt (¨-e)/die Staatsanwältin (-nen)	public prosecutor
der Rechtsanwalt (¨-e)	lawyer, barrister

A

B

Das Privatrecht

jn. verklagen
den Rechtsweg einschlagen
eine Sache vor Gericht bringen
jn. auf etw. (+Acc) verklagen
die Scheidung einreichen
sie bekam DMn Schadensersatz
  zugesprochen
die Beleidigung ⎫
die Verleumdung ⎭

Civil law

to take s.o. to court/sue
to take legal proceedings
to go to court over sth.
to sue s.o. over sth.
to sue for divorce
she was awarded DMn damages

slander, libel

C

Das öffentliche Recht

die Straftat (-en)
ein Verbrechen begehen (irreg)
kriminell leben
ein kleineres Vergehen
gegen das Gesetz verstoßen*
  (ö-ie-o)
der Vorbestrafte (adj. noun)
kriminell werden
die Bandenkriminalität
der Verbrecher (-)
der Mittäter (-)
der Einbruch (¨e)
der Einbrecher (-)
der Dieb (-e)
der Diebstahl (¨e)
stehlen (ie-a-o)
der Taschendieb (-e)
der Ladendiebstahl
einen Bankraub verüben
mit Diebesgut handeln
die Sachbeschädigung
der Vandalismus
mutwillig beschädigt
der Fussballrowdy
das Rowdytum bekämpfen
die Festnahme (-n)
jn. festnehmen
mutmaßlich

Criminal law

criminal offence
to commit a crime
to lead a life of crime
a minor offence
to break the law

person with a criminal record
to become a criminal
organised crime
criminal
accomplice
burglary
burglar
thief
theft
to steal
pickpocket
shoplifting
to commit a bank robbery
to receive stolen goods
damage to property
vandalism
damaged by vandals
football hooligan
to combat thuggery
arrest
to arrest s.o.
suspected

in Untersuchungshaft nehmen	to take into custody
die Bestechung	bribery
die Erpressung	blackmail
die Unterschlagung	embezzlement
der Betrug	fraud
die Steuerhinterziehung	tax evasion
missbrauchen	to misuse
der Datenschutz	data protection
personenbezogene Daten	personal data
in die Hände von Unbefugten gelangen (i-a-u)*	to fall into the wrong hands
schwarzarbeiten	to work without a permit, to moonlight
schwarzfahren*	to travel without a ticket/drive without a licence
die Parkkralle (-n)	wheel clamp
eine Parkkralle anlegen	to wheel-clamp
das Verkehrsdelikt (-e)	traffic offence

Die Gewalt

Violence

jn. überfallen (*insep*)	to attack, mug
der Straßenraub	mugging
die Gewalttätigkeit	violence
bewaffnet	armed
gewaltsam	by force
die Körperverletzung	grievous bodily harm
jn. zusammenschlagen	to beat s.o. up
einschüchtern	to intimidate
die Vergewaltigung	rape
entführen	to kidnap
ein Lösegeld verlangen	to demand a ransom
das Opfer (-)	victim
in Notwehr handeln	to act in self-defence
der Mord (-e) (an jm.)	murder (of s.o.)
der Mörder (-)	murderer
ermorden	to murder, assassinate
kaltblütig	in cold blood
der Schuss (-̈e)	shot
die Gewalt als Mittel der Konfliktlösung	violence as a means of dealing with conflict
auf jn. schießen	to shoot at s.o.

D

jn. erschießen	to shoot s.o. dead
er schoss sie in den Arm	he shot her in the arm

Die öffentliche Ordnung — **Public order**

die Ordnungskräfte (*pl*)	law and order
gesetzestreu	law-abiding
das Recht selbst in die Hand nehmen	to take the law into one's own hands
die Jugendkriminalität	juvenile delinquency
der jugendliche Straftäter	young offender
die Gang (-s), die Bande (-n)	gang
eine Demonstration veranstalten	to hold a demonstration
friedlich	peaceful
außer Kontrolle geraten (ä-ie-a)*	to get out of hand
die Schlägerei (-en)	(fist) fight
der Krawall (-e)	riot
etw. in Brand stecken	to set fire to sth.

Die Polizei — **Police**

die Verbrechensbekämpfung	the fight against crime
die Verbrechensrate	crime rate
die Verbrechensverhütung	crime prevention
die Null-Toleranz-Strategie	zero-tolerance strategy
die Aufklärungsquote	detection rate
das Überfallkommando	riot police
die Schutzausrüstung	riot gear
das Tränengas	tear gas
die Polizei fährt in diesem Viertel Streife	the police patrols this area
der Streifenwagen (-)	patrol car
eine Razzia (*pl* Razzien) machen	to raid, make a swoop on
die Fahndung	search
der Kriminalbeamte (*adj. noun*)	detective
die Kriminalpolizei	CID
die Kriminaltechnik	forensic science
die Fingerabdrücke (*pl*)	finger prints
das Phantombild (-er)	identikit picture
die Spur (-en)	clue
untersuchen	to investigate, search
gegen jn. ermitteln	to investigate s.o.

in einem Fall ermitteln	to investigate a case
aufspüren	to track down
ein Verbrechen aufklären	to solve a crime
verhaften	to arrest
einen Verbrecher fangen	to catch a criminal
jn. auf frischer Tat ertappen	to catch s.o. red-handed
einen Dieb fassen	to catch a thief
jn. beim Einbrechen stellen/ erwischen	to catch s.o. breaking in
jm. Handschellen anlegen	to handcuff s.o.
jn. auf das Polizeirevier bringen	to take s.o. to the police station
jn. vernehmen, verhören	to question s.o.
er bleibt in Untersuchungshaft	he's been remanded in custody
man hat sie auf Kaution freigelassen	she's out on bail
die Verbrechensverhütung	crime prevention
bei (+Dat) hart durchgreifen	to clamp down on
entkommen* (o-a-o)	to escape

Vor Gericht   **In court**

die Schöffen (pl)	jury
jn. strafrechtlich verfolgen	to prosecute s.o.
ihr Fall kam vor Gericht	her case came before the court
vor Gericht erscheinen*	to appear in court
jn. (wegen +Gen) anklagen	to charge s.o. (with)
unter Mordanklage stehen	to be on a murder charge
er wurde des Mordes angeklagt	he was charged with murder
auf der Anklagebank sitzen	to be in the dock
sich (nicht) schuldig bekennen	to plead (not) guilty
der/die Angeklagte (adj. noun)	defendant
die Anklagevertretung	counsel for the prosecution
die Verteidigung	counsel for the defence
jn. ins Kreuzverhör nehmen	to interrogate s.o.
der Zeuge (-n)/Zeugin (-nen)	witness
jn. als Zeugen vorladen	to call a witness
der Augenzeuge	eye-witness
für/gegen jn. aussagen	to give evidence for/against s.o.
das Beweismaterial	evidence
der genetische Fingerabdruck ist als Beweismittel zugelassen	genetic fingerprinting is permitted evidence
die Aussage (-n)	statement
etw. in Frage stellen	to call sth. into question

beweisen	to prove
widerlegen	to disprove
einen Meineid leisten	to commit perjury
das Verbrechen gestehen *(irreg)*	to confess to a crime
das Urteil verkünden	to pass sentence
jn. (nicht) schuldig sprechen	to find s.o. (not) guilty
jn. freisprechen	to acquit s.o.
aus Mangel an Beweisen	due to insufficient evidence
das Urteil (-e)	judgement, verdict
einen Täter überführen	to convict a criminal
die Strafe soll dem Verbrechen angemessen sein	the punishment should fit the crime
hart	severe
eine harte Linie verfolgen	to take a hard line
milde	lenient
härtere Strafen sind kein Heilmittel	harsher penalties are not the answer
jn. zu einer Geldstrafe verurteilen	to fine s.o.
der Sozialdienst	community service
sie muss 100 DM Strafe bezahlen	she's been fined DM100
die Jugendstrafanstalt (-en)	detention centre for young offenders
jn. ins Gefängnis schicken	to send s.o. to prison
der Gefangene	prisoner
überfüllt	overcrowded
ins Gefängnis kommen	to go to prison
die Zelle (-n)	cell
die lebenslängliche Freiheitsstrafe	life sentence
er wurde zu 6 Monaten Haft verurteilt	he was sentenced to 6 months imprisonment
jn. kriminalisieren	to criminalise s.o.
Berufung einlegen	to appeal
Verbrechen lohnen sich nicht	crime doesn't pay
die Wiedereingliederung	reintegration (into society)
eine mangelnde Werteorientierung	a lack of any sense of moral values

www.planet-tegel.de
www.lbb.bw.schule.de

Die Einwanderung	Immigration	A
der Einwanderer (-)	immigrant	
der Auswanderer (-)	emigrant	
der Aussiedler (-)	immigrant from former Eastern bloc countries	
der Übersiedler (-)	immigrant from former GDR	
die ehemalige DDR	what used to be the GDR	
in die BRD übersiedeln	to emigrate to the Federal Republic	
der ausländische Arbeitnehmer (-) ⎫ der Gastarbeiter (-) ⎭	foreign worker	
der Bürger (-)	citizen	
anwerben (i-a-o)	to recruit	
das Herkunftsland (-̈er)	country of origin	
die Ausreisebestimmungen lockern	to relax emigration laws	
der Ausreisewillige (*adj. noun*)	prospective emigrant	
die Freizügigkeit	freedom of movement	
das Rote Kreuz	the Red Cross	
über eine Arbeitserlaubnis verfügen	to have a work permit	
der Ausreiseantrag	application for emigration permit	
das Ausreisevisum	exit visa	
das Aufnehmeverfahren abschließen	to complete admission procedures	
er hat das Recht auf Einbürgerung in die BRD	he has the right to German citizenship	
die doppelte Staatsbürgerschaft	dual nationality	
die Arbeitsgenehmigung (-en)	work permit	
die Aufenthaltserlaubnis (-e)	residence permit	
das Aufenthaltsrecht	the right to residence	
repatriieren	to repatriate	
Eingliederungsgeld erhalten	to receive financial aid (to assist integration)	
das Notaufnahmelager (-)	reception centre, transit camp	
die Unterbringung	accommodation	
soziale Leistungen (*pl*)	social services	
integrieren	to absorb, integrate	

Die Probleme für das Gastland	Problems for the host country

das Einwanderungsland das Aufnahmeland (-er) }	host country
sie wohnen geballt in bestimmten Regionen	they live predominantly in certain areas
der Zuzug (-e)	influx
das Ghetto	ghetto
der Anteil der Ausländer an der Bevölkerung liegt bei n%	there is an immigrant population of n%
der Wirtschaft kann ausländische Arbeitskräfte nicht entbehren	the economy cannot do without foreign workers
Ehegatten folgen ihren Partnern	spouses join their partners
sie holen ihre Familien nach	they bring their families over
die soziale Integration	social integration

Die Probleme der Einwanderer	Problems for the immigrants

sich auf Deutsch mündlich verständigen können	to be able to make oneself understood in German
kulturelle Unterschiede (pl)	cultural differences
die kulturelle Identität wahren	to maintain one's cultural identity
Ausländer der zweiten Generation	second generation immigrants
vom sozialen Aufstieg ausgeschlossen	excluded from social advancement
sich abkapseln	to cut/shut oneself off
unqualifizierte Arbeit	unskilled work
niedrig	menial
die Unterschicht	the underclass
schlechtbezahlt	poorly paid
elend, erbärmlich	squalid
schlechte Wohnbedingungen	poor living conditions
von der Arbeitslosigkeit stark betroffen	badly affected by unemployment
sich einleben	to settle down
in ihre Heimat zurückkehren*	to return home
finanzielle Anreize (pl) zur Rückkehr in die Heimat die Rückkehrhilfe }	financial incentives to return home
andere Länder, andere Sitten	other countries, other customs

die Lebensart (-en)	way of life
die Herkunft	background
die Hautfarbe	skin colour

Flüchtlinge und Asylanten

Refugees and asylum seekers

das Asylrecht	the right to asylum
der Asylant/der Asylbewerber	asylum seeker
einen Asylantrag billigen/ablehnen	to approve/turn down an application for asylum
Asyl erhalten	to be granted asylum
der Flüchtling (-e)	refugee
der Vertriebene (*adj. noun*)	refugee, exile
enteignen	to expropriate, dispossess
die ethnische Minderheit	ethnic minority
Angst haben vor (*+Dat*)	to fear
die Unterdrückung	oppression
die Armut	poverty
verfolgen	to persecute
wegen ihrer politischen Überzeugung	because of their political views
die Naturkatastrophe (-n)	natural disaster
Flüchtlinge aufnehmen	to admit/absorb refugees
Asylgesetze (*pl*) verschärfen	to tighten up the law on the granting of asylum
den Zuzug von Flüchtlingen möglichst gering halten	to keep the influx of immigrants as low as possible
den Zuzug sperren	to stop the influx of immigrants
die Gleichberechtigung	equal rights
die Ungleichheit	inequality

Der Rassismus

Racism

die Ausländerfeindlichkeit	hatred of foreigners
der Rassismus	racism
die Rassendiskriminierung	racial discrimination
Rassenvorurteile (*pl*) haben	to be racially prejudiced
jn. diskriminieren	to discriminate against s.o.
sie werden wie Bürger zweiter Klasse behandelt	they are treated like second-class citizens
schikanieren	to harass, bully
terrorisieren	to terrorise

zusammenschlagen	to beat up
der Rassenkrawall (-e)	race riot
die Rassenunruhen (*pl*)	racial disturbances
der Brandanschlag (¨-e)	arson attack
wieder auftauchen	to resurface
das Wiederaufleben	resurgence
den Groll anfachen	to fuel resentment
der Neo-Nazismus	neo-Nazism
auf Rassismus zurückzuführen	racially motivated
die Eskalation	escalation
Ängste ausnutzen	to play on fears
die Überfremdung	swamping with foreigners
das Misstrauen	mistrust
die kulturelle Vielfalt	cultural diversity
die Feindseligkeit	hostility
auf beiden Seiten	on both sides
leiden unter (+*Dat*)	to suffer from
der kulturelle Konflikt	cultural clash
der Islam, islamisch	Islam, Islamic
die Moschee (-n)	mosque
der Judaismus, jüdisch	Judaism, Jewish
der Jude (-n)/Jüdin (-nen)	Jew/Jewess
der Antisemitismus	anti-Semitism
die Synagoge (-n)	synagogue
die Vergangenheitsbewältigung	coming to terms with the guilt of the past
der Glaube	faith, belief
der gläubige Mensch (-en)	believer
das Christentum	Christianity
der Christ (-en)	Christian

www.verfassungsschutz.de
www.ekd.de
www.comlink.de/cl-hh/m.blumentritt/agr.htm

Das Kulturleben

Die Musik — Music

Die Musik	Music
das Kammerorchester	chamber orchestra
der Chor (¨e)	choir, chorus, choral work
die Kapelle (-)	band (brass, etc.)
der Musiker (-)	musician
der Dirigent (-en)	conductor
dirigieren	to conduct
einstudieren	to rehearse
die Blechbläser (pl)	brass section
die Holzbläser (pl)	woodwind section
die Streicher (pl)	strings section
das Schlagzeug	percussion section
die Saite (-n)	string
der Solist (-en)	soloist
der Virtuose (-n)/die Virtuosin (-nen)	virtuoso
die Oper (-n)	opera
die Symphonie (-n)	symphony
das Konzert (-e)	concerto, concert
die Noten (pl) / die Partitur (-en)	score
die Noten (pl)	(sheet) music
das Stück (-e)	piece of music
vom Blatt spielen	to sight-read
nach Gehör spielen	to play by ear
der Komponist (-en)	composer
komponieren	to compose, write music
der Konzertsaal (-säle)	concert hall
in die Oper gehen	to go to the opera
ins Konzert gehen	to go to a concert
die zeitgenössische Musik	contemporary music
musizieren	to play a musical instrument
klingen	to sound
der Flügel (-)	grand piano
der Straßenmusikant (-en)	street musician, busker
die Band (-s)	band (pop)
die Musikbox (-en)	juke box
die Fahrstuhlmusik	canned music, muzak

B | **Die Kunst** | **Art**

die bildenden Künste (*pl*)	fine arts
der Künstler (-)	artist
das Kunstwerk (-e)	work of art
die Ausstellung (-en)	exhibition
das Gemälde (-)	painting (object)
die Malerei	painting (art form)
malen	to paint
skizzieren	to sketch
der (Mal-)Stil	style (of painting)
das Aquarell (-e)	water-colour (painting)
das Ölgemälde (-)	oil painting
das Porträt (-s)	portrait
das Meisterwerk (-e)	masterpiece
im Vordergrund	in the foreground
im Hintergrund	in the background
die Skulptur, die Bildhauerkunst	sculpture (art form)
die Skulptur (-en), die Plastik (-en)	sculpture (object)
die Statue (-n)	statue
darstellen	to represent
kitschig	trashy, posing as art
die Grafik	graphic art
entwerfen (i-a-o)	to design
die Architektur ⎫ die Baukunst ⎭	architecture
architektonisch	architectural

C | **Theater und Film** | **Theatre and film**

das Stück (-e)	play
gegeben werden*	to be on, showing
aufführen	to perform (*tr*)
auftreten*	to perform (*itr*)
die Aufführung (-en)	performance (of play)
seine Darstellung des Hamlets	his performance of Hamlet
die Generalprobe (-n)	rehearsal
eine Rolle spielen	to play a part
die Erstaufführung (-en)	first night
die Besetzung (-en)	cast
der Schauspieler (-)	actor
die Inszenierung (-en)	production

der Regisseur (-s)	director
Regie führen bei (+*Dat*)	to direct
die Bühne (-n)	stage
die Kulissen (*pl*)	wings
das Bühnenbild (-er)	set
die Beleuchtung	lighting
die Kostüme (*pl*)	costumes, wardrobe
die Pause (-n)	interval
das Laientheater	amateur dramatics
die Komödie (-n)	comedy
die Tragödie (-n)	tragedy
Subventionen erhalten	to receive subsidies
das Repertoiretheater	repertory theatre
die Zuschauer (*pl*) ⎫	
das Publikum ⎭	audience
jm. Beifall klatschen	to applaud s.o.
wir haben ein Abonnement im Theater	we have a season ticket to the theatre
der Spielplan	programme (for season)
das Programm (-e)	programme (for performance)
die Festspiele (*pl*)	festival (music, theatre, etc.)
die künstlerische Freiheit beeinträchtigen	to restrict artistic freedom
der Klassiker (-)	classic
es fand bei den Kritikern wenig Lob	it met with little praise from the critics
die Folge (-n)	sequel
ausverkauft	sold out
der Kinorenner (-)	box-office hit
der Flop (-s)	flop
durchfallen (ä-ie-a)*	flop
der Erfolg (-e)	success
anspruchsvoll	demanding
eine packende Thematik	exciting subject matter
einen Film drehen	to make a film
der Spielfilm (-e)	feature film
synchronisieren	to dub
mit deutschen Untertiteln	with German subtitles
das Drehbuch (-̈er)	screenplay
die Trailer (-s), die Vorschau	trailer
die Vorstellung (-en)	showing (of film)
die Spezialeffekte (*pl*)	special effects

Die Literatur	Literature
der Schriftsteller (-)	writer
das Werk (-e)	work
das Meisterwerk (-e)	masterpiece
gesammelte Werke (pl)	complete works
die Dichtung	literature, writing, poetry (also refers to individual work)
die Gattung (-en)	genre
das Drama	drama
die Belletristik	fiction and poetry
die Poesie	poetry
die Prosa	prose
der Roman (-e)	novel
der Bildungsroman (-e)	novel about the development of a character
der Liebesroman (-e)	romantic novel
die Erzählung (-en)	short story
der Reißer, Thriller	thriller
die Gruselgeschichte (-n)	horror story
die Novelle (-n)	novella
der Dichter (-)	poet
das Gedicht (-e)	poem
die Sammlung (-en)	collection
das Sachbuch (-̈er)	non-fiction
veröffentlichen	to publish
er erschien bei ...	it was published by ...
der Verlag (-e)	publisher
neu erschienen	recently published
das Taschenbuch (-̈er)	paperback
die gebundene Ausgabe	hardback edition
der Klappentext	blurb
der Erzähler (-)	narrator
die Erzählung	narrative
der Dialog (-e)	dialogue
eine Erzählung in der Ich-/Er-form	a story in the first/third person
es spielt in ...(+Dat)	it is set in ...
der Schauplatz der Erzählung	the scene of the story
die Handlung (-en)	plot
die Nebenhandlung (-en)	sub-plot
sich entfalten	to unfold (itr)
entfalten	to unfold (tr)

entwickeln	to develop (*tr*)
die Gestalt (-en)	character (person, figure)
der Charakter (-)	character (personality)
die Charakterisierung	characterisation
die Eigenschaft (-en)	characteristic
menschliche Beziehungen (*pl*)	human relationships
sein Verhältnis zu seiner Frau	his relationship with his wife
der Vorgang (¨-e)	event
der Ausgang	ending
das Happy-End	happy end
schließlich	in the end
beschreiben	to describe
darstellen ⎫ schildern ⎭	to portray
erzählen	to recount
der Aufstieg	the rise
der Verfall	the fall
erfunden	imaginary
die Phantasie	imagination
sich (*Dat*) etw. vorstellen	to imagine sth.
die Lehre (-n)	moral point
die Trümmerliteratur	literature of the immediate post-war years
die Frauenliteratur	books by women
verarbeiten	to deal with (subject)
es behandelt die Frage ...	it deals with the question of ...
es dreht sich um ... (*+Acc*)	it concerns, is about ...
handeln von (*+Dat*)	to be about
es setzt sich kritisch mit ... auseinander (*+Dat*)	it takes a critical look at ...
ein starkes gesellschaftliches Engagement	a strong social conscience
eine moralisch fundierte Sozialkritik	social criticism with a basis in morality
die Schattenseiten (*pl*) des Wirtschaftswunders	the down side to the economic miracle
das Unbehagen an ...(*+Dat*)	unease, disquiet at ...
das Misstrauen gegen ...(*+Acc*)	mistrust of ...
der Materialismus	materialism
es artikuliert sich in ...(*+Dat*)	it is expressed in ...
etw. in Frage stellen	to question sth.

zum Thema werden	to become an issue
ein zentrales Thema	a central theme
eine Reflexion über ... (+Acc)	a reflection on ...
eine kritische Einstellung zu ... (+Dat)	a critical attitude to ...
kompromisslos	uncompromising
die Nöte und Sorgen der kleinen Leute	the problems and worries of ordinary people
das menschliche Scheitern	human failure

E

Die Literaturkritik / Literary criticism

die Zusammenfassung	summary
der Kommentar (-e)	commentary
die Kritik	critique, criticism
analysieren	to analyse
vermitteln	to convey
vergleichen	to compare
ausdrücken	to express
erklären	to explain
zitieren	to quote
das Zitat (-e)	quotation
auf etw. (+Acc) reagieren	to react to sth.
was können wir daraus entnehmen?	what can we draw/infer from this?

1 Positives / Positive points

der Ideenreichtum	inventiveness
ideenreich	imaginative
gefühlstief	intense
gefühlvoll	sensitive
lebensnah	true to life
wir fühlen uns in seine Lage hineinversetzt	we imagine ourselves in his position
spannend	exciting
aktionsreich	action-packed
lebendig	vivid
unterhaltsam, kurzweilig	entertaining
glaubwürdig	believable
aufwühlend	disturbing
beachtlich	relevant, excellent
humorvoll, heiter	humorous

ergreifend, rührend	moving
fesselnd	gripping
sehr lesenswert	worth reading
leicht verständlich	easily understood
liebevoll	affectionate
optimistisch	optimistic
witzig	witty
glanzvoll	sparkling
warmherzig	warm-hearted
einer der bedeutendsten Romane	one of the most significant novels
die Einfühlung in (+Acc)	empathy with
stimmungsvoll	full of atmosphere
wirkungsvoll	effective
zeitlos	timeless
zutreffend	accurate
konsequent durchdacht	well thought out

2 Negatives

Negative points

weitausholend	long-winded
verwickelt ⎫ kompliziert ⎭	involved, convoluted
das Klischee (-s)	cliché
voller Klischees	full of clichés
klischeehaft	stereotyped
plump	crude, obvious
unglaubwürdig	unbelievable
vage	vague
skurril	scurrilous
simpel	simplistic
banal	banal
belanglos	trivial
monoton	repetitive
trist	drab
enttäuschend	disappointing
zusammenhanglos	disjointed
mittelmäßig	mediocre
unlogisch	illogical
dürftig	insubstantial
schwer zu lesen	unreadable
unverständlich	incomprehensible

3 Neutrales	*Neutral points*
ausführlich	detailed
kühl, distanziert	detached, impersonal
ironisch	ironic
realistisch	realistic
didaktisch	didactic, with a message
idealistisch	idealistic
nostalgisch	nostalgic
sentimental	sentimental
es stellt hohe Ansprüche an den Leser	it makes great demands on the reader
anspruchsvoll	demanding, highbrow
anspruchslos	undemanding, lowbrow
ernsthaft	serious
verzweifelt	despairing
pessimistisch	pessimistic
rührselig	sentimental
brutal	violent
wir bekommen dadurch einen Einblick in ... (+Acc)	it gives us an insight into ...
zusammenschließen (ie-o-o)	to combine, bring together

www.
www.gutenberg.aol.de
www.deutsche-kultur-international.de
www.epo.de
www.de.dir.yahoo.com/Unterhaltung/Musik/
www.sound.de
www.hithaus.de

Welches Wort soll ich wählen?

The following are a selection of key words in English to help you choose the most appropriate German equivalent.

after

nach (+Dat) (*preposition*)
nachdem (*conjunction*)
nachher (*adverb*)

nach der Pause ...
Nachdem der Film zu Ende war, ...
..., und nachher ging er ins Café

to appear, seem, look

aussehen (=*have the appearance of*)
scheinen (=*seem*)
erscheinen* (=*appear in view*)
auftauchen* (=*appear after absence*)

Er sieht krank aus.
Sie scheint ihn zu kennen.
Er ist in der Tür erschienen.
Gestern tauchte er bei uns auf.

to ask

fragen (nach +Dat) (=*to ask a
   question about*)
eine Frage stellen (=*ask a question*)
bitten (um +Acc) (=*to ask for sth.*)

Ich fragte ihn nach seiner Mutter.

Er stellt eine Frage.
Der Lehrer bittet um Ruhe.

before

vor (+Dat) (*preposition*)
before (*conjunction*)
zuvor (*adverb*)

vor dem Film ...
Bevor der Film angefangen hat, ...
ein paar Tage zuvor

to care, be careful

vorsichtig (=*cautious*)
sorgfältig (=*painstaking*)
sorgen für (+Acc) (=*look after,
   provide for*)
es ist mir egal (='*I don't care*')

Bei Schnee vorsichtig fahren!
Er lernt alles sorgfältig.
Wir sorgen für unsere Kinder.

Es ist mir egal, ob ...

to catch

fangen (=*to trap, catch, hold*)

erreichen (=*just catch e.g. a train*)

einen Fisch/Ball/eine Erkältung
   fangen
Erreichst du den Zug noch?

115

to enjoy

(jm.) gefallen (=to be pleased with)	Diese Musik gefällt mir sehr!
sich amüsieren (=have a good time)	Amüsiert euch gut!
Spaß an etw. (+Dat) haben (=get pleasure from)	Er hat Spaß an seinem Oldtimer.
Spaß machen (=be fun)	Der Abend hat uns Spaß gemacht.
genießen (=to savour)	einen guten Wein genießen

to feel

fühlen/empfinden (=to feel/sense)	Furcht/Hunger empfinden
sich fühlen (=to feel +adverb)	Ich fühle mich krank/unglücklich.

to get Think of a synonym; a few of the many possibilities are:

werden* (=become)	Ich werde alt.
haben (=own)	Sie hat ihr erstes Auto.
bekommen (=receive)	Ich bekam heute einen Brief.
sich (+Dat) etw. anschaffen/besorgen (=buy, obtain)	Ich muss mir einen Computer anschaffen/besorgen.
verdienen (=earn)	Sie verdient ein gutes Gehalt.

to know

kennen (=be familiar with)	jn./eine Stadt kennen
wissen (=by learning/experience)	Weißt du die Lösung?

to learn

lernen (by study)	Sie lernt Italienisch.
erfahren (=find out)	Ich erfuhr die Wahrheit.

to leave

(liegen)lassen (=leave [behind])	Ich ließ alles zu Hause (liegen).
verlassen (=quit)	Ich verlasse das Haus um 8.
abfahren* (=set off)	Wir fahren um 8 ab.
überlassen (=let s.o. see to)	Überlass es mir!

to look (see also: appear)

etw. ansehen (=look at)	Sie sah sein Foto liebevoll an.
sich (+Dat) etw. ansehen (=have a look at)	Ich will mir die Welt ansehen.
sehen auf (=glance at)	Ich sah auf meine Uhr.

number

die Nummer (of house, phone)	die Nummer meines Hauses
die Zahl (mathematical)	ein gutes Gedächtnis für Zahlen
die Anzahl (indefinite)	eine große Anzahl von Problemen

only
erst (=*not before* +*time*)   Ich kann erst um 8 kommen.
nur (=*no more than* +*quantity*)   Ich habe nur wenig Zeit.
einzige (*adj*) (=*single*)   Er ist der einzige, der da war.

people
die Leute (*pl*) (=*group of people*)   Sie sind sehr nette Leute.
die Menschen (*pl*) (=*people in*   Alle Menschen müssen sterben.
  general)
die Personen (*pl*) (=*individuals*)   eine Familie aus 6 Personen
das Volk (=*nation*)   das deutsche Volk
viele (=*many people*)   Viele sind der Meinung, dass ...

to put
legen (=*lying down*)   Er legte das Buch auf den Tisch.
stellen (=*standing*)   Stell die Flasche auf den Tisch!
stecken (=*put into*)   Er steckt die Hand in die Tasche.
tun (*in general – colloquial*)   Tu die Tassen in den Schrank!

to stop
halten (*itr*) (=*halt*)   Der Bus hält hier.
anhalten (*tr/itr*) (*temporary,*   Plötzlich hielt er das Auto an.
  unexpected)
aufhalten (*tr*) (=*delay, hinder*)   Der Streik hält den Brief auf.
aufhören (*itr*) (=*stop doing sth.*)   Es hörte auf zu regnen.

to stay
bleiben (=*remain in one*   Er blieb den ganzen Tag bei uns.
  place/condition)
wohnen/sich aufhalten   Er hält sich im Hotel auf.
  (=*be based temporarily*)
verbringen (=*spend time*)   Ich verbringe 3 Tage in den USA.
übernachten (=*stay the night*)   Du kannst bei uns übernachten.

to take
nehmen (=*pick up, use*)   Nimm den Zug/dieses Buch!
bringen (*someone somewhere*)   Ich bringe dich zum Bahnhof.
dauern (*time*)   Die Reise hat 2 Stunden gedauert.

there is/are (*Much less used in German than English. Avoid where possible.*)
es gibt (*general*)   Es gibt einen Gott. (Gott existiert.)
es ist/sind (*specific time, place*)   Es ist ein Mann im Auto. (Ein Mann
                                                   sitzt ...)

thing
die Sache (-n) (=*possession*)
  (=*affair, subject*)

das Ding (*object*)
  (*pl.* =*serious matters*)
  + adjective
überhaupt nichts
seinen eigenen Weg gehen

to think
denken an (=*have in mind*)
denken/halten von (=*have an
  opinion on*)
halten für (=*consider to be*)
nachdenken über (=*weigh up*)

meinen (=*give an opinion*)

time
die Zeit (-en) (*period*)
das Mal (-e) (*occasion*)
jm. Spaß machen (*a good time*)

to try
versuchen (=*attempt*)
probieren (=*sample*)
an-/ausprobieren (=*try on/out*)

to use
benutzen, verwenden (=*to utilize*)

gebrauchen (=*utilize sth. one has*)
nutzen (=*to exploit, positive*)
ausnutzen (=*to exploit, negative*)
anwenden (=*to apply*)
verbrauchen (=*to consume*)

to work
arbeiten (=*labour*)
funktionieren, gehen (=*function*)
klappen (=*to work out*) (*inf.*)
ausdenken (*to work out scheme*)

Hast du deine Sachen mit?
Sport ist nicht meine Sache/
  mein Ding.
Was ist das für ein Ding?
Diese Dinge gehen nur mich an.
Das Beste/Schlimmste ist, ...
not a thing
to do one's own thing

Woran denkst du?
Was hältst du von ihm?

Ich halte es für das Beste, wenn ...
Wir müssen darüber nachdenken,
  ob ...
Ich meine, es wäre besser, wenn ...

Ich habe keine Zeit dazu.
Sie ist zum ersten Mal hier.
Es hat mir Spaß gemacht!

Ich versuchte, ihm zu helfen.
Probieren Sie diesen Wein!
Hast du diese Methode ausprobiert?

Ich benutze immer ein
  Wörterbuch.
Er gebraucht einen Kuli.
Sie nutzt jede Chance.
Er nutzt ihre Gutmütigkeit aus.
Sie hat diese Methode angewandt.
Ein großes Auto verbraucht viel
  Benzin.

Sie hat sich nach oben gearbeitet.
Meine Uhr geht nicht.
Ich hoffe, dass es klappt.
Ich muss mir einen Plan ausdenken.